THE
LAST SCROLL

A GUIDING LIGHT TO WISDOM

TERRY LEE MCCLAIN

Gotham Books

30 N Gould St.
Ste. 20820, Sheridan, WY 82801
https://gothambooksinc.com/

Phone: 1 (307) 464-7800

© 2023 *Terry Lee McClain*. All rights reserved.

No part of this book may be reproduced, stored in a retrieval system, or transmitted by any means without the written permission of the author.

Published by Gotham Books (November 1, 2023)

ISBN: 979-8-88775-609-7 (P)
ISBN: 979-8-88775-610-3 (E)

Because of the dynamic nature of the Internet, any web addresses or links contained in this book may have changed since publication and may no longer be valid.

The views expressed in this work are solely those of the author and do not necessarily reflect the views of the publisher, and the publisher hereby disclaims any responsibility for them.

TABLE OF CONTENTS

DEDICATIONS VII
ACKNOWLEDGMENTS VIII
INTRODUCTION IX
CHAPTER 1 The Beginning 1
CHAPTER 2 The Trunk 6
CHAPTER 3 Boot Camp and beyond 12
CHAPTER 4 Eight n Nine 16
CHAPTER 5 The Test 21
CHAPTER 6 Pure Love 29
CHAPTER 7 The Wise One 35
CHAPTER 8 The Last Scroll 38
CHAPTER 9 The Reunion 40
CHAPTER 10 The Author Talks 42
CHAPTER 11 What the Scriptures Say Not Me 47
CHAPTER 12 Pushing Forward 50
CHAPTER 13 Time is moving on 53
CHAPTER 14 Play Time Is Over 59
CHAPTER 15 Common Sense 62
CHAPTER 16 Where to Next 66
CHAPTER 17 Stay Humble 72
CHAPTER 18 Attachments 74
CHAPTER 19 Better Times 78

CHAPTER 20 Temptations 80

CHAPTER 21 Getting Through 83

CHAPTER 22 Hold Your Head Up High 86

CHAPTER 23 The Going Away 89

CHAPTER 24 Good and Evil 93

CHAPTER 25 Acceptance 97

CHAPTER 26 Encouragement 104

CHAPTER 27 Best Chance 107

CHAPTER 28 Days Ahead 111

CHAPTER 29 Learn to Be Alright 114

DEDICATIONS

To my daddy, Robbie Lee McClain (RIP). My mother, Sallie Ann Ross-McClain (Feb 25,1944 - June 17, 2018) (RIP). To the living, my fiancée (Deneen) for her unconditional love for me and for supporting me during the journey to write this novel. Also, to all of my grandchildren (Ariah Melody McClain, Cassidy Connor, Duriel Connor "Little Man", London McClain, and Royalty McClain). Finally, to the people still in active addiction (I pray that you seek help) and to the children around the world

ACKNOWLEDGMENTS

I want to thank the Lord, Jesus Christ for the countless blessings He has bestowed upon me and for giving me the gift of writing. Also, I wish to acknowledge my publisher Gotham Books Inc. and Audrey Monroe with a personal and special thanks. For they have given me the very best of their services. I especially thank Gotham Books Inc. for giving me the opportunity to reveal my writings. Again, thank you Gotham Books Inc.

INTRODUCTION

Today, (Wednesday) November 29, 2017. My morning has begun in a spectacular fashion. I am feeling my best. I feel as though I am at the pinnacle of a point in my life that defies my own understanding. Mentally, physically, and spiritually I could not feel better about my existence here on earth. Truly, the portion of the scriptures (The King James version) where in Psalms 23 verse 5 it speaks of his cup runs over. I am a living witness that life for me right now is as though there is a cup sitting inside my stomach and it is running over with good fortune. I am ecstatic about pressing on through this day! Surly, I know not what lies ahead for today. I will enjoy it though as it elapses into another glorious sunset; assured that at the closing thereof it was the will of God performing its power to fulfill everything that transpired within.

The Thanksgiving Holiday was just days ago and it all went well. We (My fiancée, her two sons, daughter/w husband, two grand-children and their mother) had dinner together at our house early; eleven thirty or noon or so. After dinner, we took pictures (taken by my nephew Roger "Scooter" McClain of whom is transforming into one of the best photographers in the world), laughed, and talked for a while. We began to separate in order to visit other family members. With their carry-out plates packed. Everyone took off to different destinations. We had a gracious, blessed, and thankful good time together at our house to begin the festivities of the day. The memories of times like these never seem to fade away. I definitely cherish every moment of these happy times.

We all begin to disperse. As I walked casually up my driveway, my biological family members started pulling up in two different vehicles. One brother/w wife and two boys, my momma, and one of two of my uncles left on my momma's side of the family (Woodrow or "Fireball"). I gave my uncle the nickname "Fireball" when I was just a small boy, because every time he came home after a night on the town his eyes would be red like fire. His family has called him "Fireball" since that time (the 80's) up until this very day. We all decided to go over one of my other brothers houses across town from where I reside here in Gastonia NC. I have six brothers and two of them reside in Lowell NC. Therefore, we all headed to the house of my youngest brother.

The house was filled with the smell of Thanksgiving Day food. We all went in and proceeded to eat, laugh, and talk among ourselves. Later, we all left and went to gather at my other brother's house (Robert Rogers McClain) of whom also resides in Lowell NC. Again, we ate, laughed, and talked for several hours. I could not help myself from absorbing the bliss of the occasion. Therefore, the day ended in laughter, giggles, and several full stomachs.

The days after Thanksgiving went well also. I went to the Veterans Hospital in Charlotte NC on November 30, 2017 for a Colonoscopy procedure. The procedure went as I anticipated; very well. The results were negative for virtually everything. I was elated! Therefore, I know for sure that my health is at least up to par. And, that is counted to me as a blessing from the Good Master above.

The Christmas Holidays are slowly approaching and again, I am anticipating a wonderful time with family and friends. It will be once again the day of the birth of our Lord Jesus Christ. I am truly very excited!

CHAPTER 1
The Beginning

Eugene Moses was now twenty-one years old and life could not be more stupendous. He was a slim type man about five feet-eight inches or five feet-nine inches tall, muscular build from his days of wrestling in high school, short black hair and brown eyes. His appearance was sharp with eyes appearing to look as though he was focused on conquering the world.

He was employed by one of the local textile companies of which was plentiful in the area in which he resided. It all began in 1981, a time in Kings Mountain North Carolina, Bessemer City North Carolina, Shelby North Carolina and Gastonia North Carolina when the average working man could walk away from a job at 8:30 a.m. and be employed again by 12:01 p.m.; in the same day. It was just an era in history when landing a job was easy as cutting a lemon pie. He resided in the small town of Kings Mountain North Carolina. A town with an old Western day town appearance and feel as though it was aged like a fine wine. Farming and textiles were the bread and butter for nearly every family in the town and perhaps the entire county (Cleveland). The farmers thrived on raising pigs, cows, and growing hay. While the textile workers thrived on the production of cotton products. Nestled between Charlotte North Carolina and Shelby North Carolina, Kings Mountain North Carolina was truly a country town.

Eugene Moses had everything going in his favor. The unseen forces beyond earth were really manifesting their powers through him to acquire materialistic treasures. He acquired virtually everything a young man could dream of; especially a black man. He had a beautiful 1976 Monte Carlo. It was pearl white with the burgundy half vinyl top and burgundy interior. Also, it had the original factory hub caps (very popular during this era) and he had installed a Sanyo stereo with six by nine Sanyo speakers. The Sanyo stereo was a top-of-the-line system at this time (very loud with virtually no distortion). Eugene had top of the line clothing, own apartment with new furniture, very few friends, a girlfriend, and financial security. Eugene had amassed a small fortune from working for different cotton mill companies. All by the time he was eighteen or nineteen years of age (virtually unheard of by a young black kid in the area in which he lived). Nevertheless, with the world in the palm of his hands; he did not know the true value of his worth; he was never introduced to the business world while growing up. His parents were very poor and virtually uneducated. Therefore, there was no reason to discuss financial matters as far as how to secure one's future by saving and risk taking. His family, (included four or five brothers with both parents) was barely surviving; virtually from day to day and even moment by moment. He was the oldest of his brothers.

By now, Eugene had developed skills to draw mechanical drawings. He learned the craft from drafting classes offered at his high school (Kings Mountain High School). His teacher was named Mr. Guy. Eugene became a master of the craft. His yearning to draw was like a baby yearning for milk.

After high school he enrolled into a local community college. Not having any sure path to follow. He just somehow knew that he wanted to continue drawing mechanical drawings. Therefore, he enrolled into a two-year program called Mechanical and Production Engineering. He was ecstatic to be a part of something again that allowed him to continue to master his skills at drawing. He continued to work in cotton mills during the evening hours and was attending college during the daytime hours. He had a full schedule for sure and was adding more to his cup; his cup was actually running over.

In 1984 Eugene became twenty-one years of age and was seemingly rising to the pinnacle of success. Every aspect of his life was gleaming like rays from a well-polished diamond. The only thing standing in his way to destined success was man, God, and himself. He was single and living the life of a Middle Eastern King.

Although He had experimented with beer and marijuana it had not affected any aspect of his life. A beer here and a beer there, a toke here and a toke there was all it ever consisted of at this point in his life. And that was done mostly in the presence of a close college friend while at the car wash.

September of 1984, he joined the Navy. At the time, the Navy was accepting volunteers with college backgrounds. They offered Eugene a job in an Engineering unit that was highly respected. When the recruiter mentioned engineering, he leaped inside himself for joy. The opportunity to draw again pierced through his mind and heart like an arrow shot from the bow of an Indian. He was elated at the opportunity presented to him and after little thought; he happily and proudly accepted the offer.

September 28,1984 was a rejuvenating type of day. It was the day he was to officially begin his sworn duty to the United States Navy. The Plane released itself from the runway at Charlotte Douglas Airport with a light force against his body. He had never flown before. Therefore, the experience was of surprise and uncertainty. Although, he had cast out of himself all doubt, fear, and nerviness of riding on an airplane days before. Because, with or without fear; he knew there was no turning back now. Destiny for him now was California and basic training for the US military. All fear had vanished from his heart, mind, and soul. He was determined to become an upstanding soldier, at virtually any cost; even if the cost would be his life.

Something inside him just gave him the feeling that failure at anything was never going to be an option; to succeed at something was his every hope, aspiration, and dream. To make his parents and his brothers proud of him was his ultimate quest. He believed that his existence would be for naught if maximum success was not achieved for his life.

Five and one-half hours later the plane glided toward the Los Angeles International Airport (L.A.X) and touched down with a light thump onto the ground like an eagle settling down upon his nest. The ride was stupendous throughout; from the beginning to the end thereof. Although, he was in another time zone everything was going great. Once inside the terminal he and other potential soldiers was swiftly escorted onto a bus. The bus reminded him of the school buses he rode on during his elementary and high school days; there was very little difference between the two. When he reached his destination on the military base he and the others was shown where they would sleep for the night. All the excitement was exhausting to the mind, body, and soul. It was one or two o'clock in the morning and he was spent. No worth to anyone left in him. Finally, they were all given a military bunk to sleep on for the night and the day was all said and done.

CHAPTER 2
The Trunk

The morning started off great. Breakfast consisted of Sausage, eggs, grits, toast, and coffee. It was Saturday 2014; a day in July when there is a plethora of yard sales scattered all over Gastonia, North Carolina. He left home this particular morning with the intentions of finding something invaluable. It was just a feeling at first; maybe just another typical Saturday. The feeling grew in intensity more and more. Eugene was puzzled, he had never had this type of feeling before. It was as though some force was instigating his senses to roam the city hunting yard sales. Again, it puzzled him. These was the times when by himself he could concentrate on the good thoughts going through his mind. The thought of how free he really was in this country (USA); for one. Two, the thoughts of how well his marriage to Gloria was progressing; overwhelming.

He loved her and that was the epitome of his feelings. And three, how well his three children were doing. Bryan was nineteen and progressively and positively approaching manhood and working on a degree in Civil Engineering at The University of North Carolina at Charlotte (UNCC). He was a sophomore and doing quite well. He was exceptionally proud of his son's accomplishments at this juncture of his life. Travis was thirteen and growing like a plant on Miracle Growth. He was beginning to feel himself too. He enjoyed impressing girls. He hoarded a plethora of friends. Cali was now nine, she was the spoiled one of the three. She loved her mom; seemingly a little too much. She loved him too. Although, he was not in her presence as much as he needed to be. He knew he had a little work still left to do in that area. Growing girls was not his best subject. They had all dispersed earlier this particular morning. And finally, how well his career was proceeding. His field had always been Engineering. Now, as a Mechanical Engineer for a company that produced mechanical components for major hospitals; he could not ask of too many more blessings of the Deity.

The house, more of an estate was a sure sign of upper middle class. Cars lined both sides of the street. The housing development was named Huntington Forest. The house was along a street named Hickory Hollow Rd. The front yard was beaming with yard sellers. The scene was like the crowds at a flea market. People was seemingly everywhere. Eugene walked a little way to the mingled crowd and began to look around. He was the type of man that automatically knew what he was searching for when out-and-about like this. He was not difficult to make deals with either. He picked up a couple of kitchen cloths for Gloria and three silver containers for the kitchen as well. The three containers would be beautiful on the kitchen counter. They were made to hold flour, sugar, and whatever else one may want to put therein. He walked down the driveway a few more feet and around to where the garage was. The sign down the street said, Big Garage Sale. Therefore, he walked on into the garage. It did not take long to notice what he was feeling earlier. The suit case was at the back of the garage. It was green with gold plated steel on the corners. He knew the gold was not real; it was scratched through to the exposed steel. The suit case was of some type of paste board. He could see the cracks in it that was seemingly racing off in thousands of directions toward infinity. He also noticed that age had waved its wand upon it as well. The black leather handle was still in great shape though; it was genuine leather for sure. He quickly went and retrieved one of the hosts and asked her if it was for sale. She looked at it and said, I don't know with a southern accent. She said, it was my husbands and he has been dead for ten years or so. Eugene said, have you thought about getting rid of it. She said, how much will you give me for it. He glanced the case over again and said, what about twenty dollars. She said, sure! It would have rotted over there anyway. She said, you know, I never have known what was in that old suit case anyhow. Eugene reached in his left front pocket and withdrew some cash. He asked the woman how much he owed her? She looked over what he had gathered up and told him twenty-six dollars. He reached her thirty dollars and she went to retrieve his change. She returned with his change and she said, thank you; I hope you enjoy your stuff. He picked up the suit case and headed back toward his car. He popped the trunk and put everything therein.

Once inside the cabin of his car. He noticed that the feeling he had earlier was now gone. He now had a feeling of calmness; like everything was alright. He drove around to a few more yard sales; found nothing of interest and returned home. It was close to noon and the wife and kids had not returned. He had the house to himself; a very rare occasion. He retrieved his items from the trunk of his car and put the trunk/suit case in the garage and took the other items in the house. The trunk had a key entry lock that had no key; nor was it locked. He never opened it.

He walked to the counter and put the other items he had bought down and went through the mail. There was nothing in the mail that drew his immediate attention. He made his way to the living room and sat down in his recliner and while relaxing; fell off to sleep. The night before in Asheville North Carolina at Harrah's Cherokee Casino had taken all his energy for now. He went to Harrah's with his work friends every Friday night; despite the fussing from Gloria. It was just his personal thing. At Harrah's, the girls, booze, and gambling were to him the epitome of having fun. There was nothing to compare it too. Keno was his game of choice. The near zero possibility of a great outcome was what excited him. The game was difficult to conquer and that was another aspect of the game he loved about it. The adrenaline rush was like diving from a bridge attached to a bungee cord. It was the epitome of self-satisfaction. No other game compared to it in his thinking; no other.

Gloria and the kids returned home after an hour or so and wanted to have grilled out food. They had retrieved all that was needed. Hot dogs, Spare ribs, Hamburgers, and center cut pork chops- the center cuts was his favorite. He got up from the recliner and started to help prepare the food for the grill.

After the food was devoured, they all set down to look at college football. Clemson and Alabama were at it again. The score near the end of the first quarter was ten to seven Clemson.

During the game Eugene rummaged through his mind, what would he do without his family. He loved them so much and could not fathom what his life would be compared to without them. They were laughing and talking together while enjoying the game. The house had the feeling of Christmas time. He chuckled to himself and his thinking went to something else. He had life by the throat and was happily embracing every moment of pleasure it was giving him. To him it seemed as though he was standing on top of the world and spinning the universe around in the palm of his hand.

Later that evening, Eugene and some work friends gathered at a local bar and had a few drinks. He had somehow noticed that his drinking of alcoholic beverages had increased to phenomenal heights. He was not to the point of having black-outs or anything of that nature. Although, it seemed to be getting out of hand. He first started off with just a couple of beers; now he was taking shots of liquor like elementary kids drinking milk. He dismissed it all in his thoughts and continued to have fun with his friends.

The bar was at the point of closing. He left his friends and returned home. His only friend that did not drink was Tony Glenn. Tony drove him home and he retired for the night. He was to attend church tomorrow and knew he needed a head start on getting prepared. He fell off to sleep peacefully behind Gloria.

CHAPTER 3
Boot Camp and beyond

The metal trash can battered the floor with an intensifying sound. The noise was deafening to the ear drums. His nerves were rattled to a crescendo his mind had never before summoned. It was about four in the morning. He was quickly awakened by the horrendous sound of the metal trash can bouncing across the concrete floor. His mind and every fiber of his body went from zero to three-hundred miles per hour in an instant. The entire world was swirling around in his head. They were all ordered to their feet and to stand at the foot of the racks. The guy yelling at the uttermost ability of his lungs was in charge; no one else could have been. After the yelling finally ceased, they all was marched to breakfast. Reality suddenly dawned on him; he was really in the military.

The next three months was basically the same routine. On your feet early and very little sleep. The days seemed endless to him.

Finally, Eugene graduated from boot camp and went on to his training schools. He was recruited to become an electrician. He completed all his schools earlier than expected, which was very impressive to the upper echelon. Everything was falling into place like a thousand-piece puzzle. He was well liked by his peers and his life seem to have meaning. He had the feeling that nothing could stop him from becoming the man he expected to become; very important.

His time in service ended sooner than he expected though; due to an injury. He was hospitalized for having black outs and never returned to his duties. He was medically discharged after one- and one-half years of active-duty service. His enlistment was for five years. He was completely devastated by the military decisions made on his behalf. It all changed his life forever; forever.

He moved back to North Carolina with his parents in 1986. A year later, life did not seem to be that difficult to live through. He eventually was introduced to Gloria through a friend and his world was all good again. He found new friends and continued to drink. Life seemed to be going his way again and that feeling was gratifying to him. Although, drinking was affecting his ability to maintain a perfect life style. Nevertheless, he continued on with his days through life. The drinking had started in college. It was at its maximum now and he could not stop. Beer was his drink of choice. By drinking he could feel comfortable around other people and most of all; he could fit in. fitting in was important to him, because while growing up he seemed to never fit in. He was a loner as they say. Now, he had confidence and could fit in anywhere he went. It was a great feeling. Although, he knew his financial situation was beginning to slide left of him. He had the mentality that if his primary bills were paid then everything else would be alright too. Although, reality was sinking in that he was going broke. Nevertheless, it was now the year 2014 and Gloria did not have a clue that his financial situation was near the point of destruction. Harrah's was not paying off right now and there was nothing he could do about it. It was just that plain and simple. It was just the nature of taking risk; sometimes you win and a majority of the time you lose. He was throwing knifes back and forth with reality. He knew the odds all so well too. He knew that sooner or later reality would score. His only hope now was that the knife of reality did not land in his heart. To lose Gloria and what he had accomplished thus far would be a complete devastation to his life. He was in a quandary.

He married Gloria in 1987. The wedding was breath taking. The four-layer cake with pink icing was awesomely beautiful along with her white dress and sparkling jewel laced necklace. The scene was like the movie scene of the wedding in the movie "Scarface". Although, their wedding had no resemblance as to mimic the movie whatsoever. It all just seemed to appear as though the scene was from a movie (a fairy tale of some sort). The reception was classic; nothing too fancy. The dancing and music were stupendous. The reception lasted until the early morning hours. The honeymoon was four days at Virginia Beach at the Hampton Inn. The fond memories would remain in his head the rest of his life.

CHAPTER 4
Eight n Nine

Dennis Morgan was twenty-three years old. He had a slight touch of autism. He knew virtually everything about dinosaurs; by name and appearance. He was well known around the neighborhood of Huntington Forest and the city of Gastonia, North Carolina. The policeman of Gastonia loved him. Eight-n-Nine got his nickname by selling various items to people. He would sell virtually anything he came upon. He sold toys, books, Christmas ornaments, shoes, electronics, women purses, and small appliances. Things just seem to drop from the sky into his hands. Eight-n-Nine would sell his momma if she dropped their last name. Everything he sold was for Eight or Nine dollars; depending upon if he knew you or not. He sold items to anybody; anybody. He did not see people for the color of their skin. The only color Eight-n-

Nine saw was green. He did not care who you were or where you came from. All that interested Eight-n-Nine was if a person had green money. He could count money and that was the only thing that ever interested him. He stayed with his parents. He had his own room upstairs of their two-story house. His parents loved him and took care of him to a phenomenal magnitude. He had his own vehicle too. A blue 2004 ford F-150. Eight-n Nine was the talk of the town as people would say. Bright and jovial at all times. Eight-n-Nine knew he was one of a kind; a class act.

Eight-n-Nine knocked at the door and rang the doorbell too. Eugene came rushing to the door with swift and precise movement. He said, hey Eight-n-Nine. Eight-n-Nine said, how you doing Mr. Moses. I got something you might need today. Eugene always respected Eight-n-Nine; he was even fond of him. Therefore, he was always patient with him. Eugene even admired him for his personal endeavors. He had to give it to ole Eight-n-Nine; the guy knew how to hustle. He knew too that there was something not quite right about Eight-n-Nine; His meter just did not turn fast. He said, what you got this time Eight-n-Nine? Eight-n-Nine said, I got a book here I found. He looked at the cover and name of the book. The title was called The Christ Commission by Og Mandino. He turned the book over and glanced at the back. He asked Eight-n-Nine, where did you get this book? Eight-n-Nine said, I found it among some things Mrs. Madlin gave me. He said, yea I know Mrs. Madlin. He said, Okay Eight-n-Nine I will buy it. How much do you want for it? Eight-n-Nine said, since

I know you Mr. Moses it will be eight dollars. Eugene reached into his right front pocket and retrieved some cash. He handed Eight-n-Nine eight dollars. Eight-n-Nine smiled with a look of gratefulness and said, Thanks Mr. Moses I appreciate that. He turned and headed for his truck. He waved again with a huge smile and said, thanks again Mr. Moses as he drove away.

The book was of fair size; not too thick and not too thin. Eugene walked over to his recliner and laid the book on the floor beside it. He said to himself, I will read it later. He returned to the kitchen counter and retrieved his mail. The bills were stacking themselves on top of each other and there seemed to be no quick solution. He knew in the forefront of his mind that something had to happen soon. Perhaps a big win at Harrah's. He had won before and was confident that he could do it again. He rummaged through all the mail and laid it all back on the counter. He went back to his recliner and retrieved the book on the floor beside it. He sat down and began to read the book Eight-n-Nine had sold him earlier; The Christ Commission.

He was hooked to the story from word one. He could not put the book down. The beginning was stupendous. Every word and every page were astonishing to him. The subject was outstanding. It was about Jesus Christ and his presence with mankind while on earth. Astounding reading material. He was captured and he knew he would finish the book. He stopped reading after a couple hundred pages or so and sat in amazement as to what was revealed to him thus far in the story.

In his mind he began to think. He had always been around religion and religious people. He grew up in a Baptist family and had studied many World Religion courses while in college. He never thought about it often (religion); he just had always believed in what was said about the man Jesus Christ. There was never a time he could remember that he truly thought about being saved or if heaven and hell was real. He only followed and believed like everyone else; go to church on Sunday and be good to everyone. He really thought that was all there was to it. His mind was thinking deeply now and the book he had just laid down had him now thinking deeper. He read the Bible here and there. That was about the jest of it. He had never been interested in religious matters to the point of reading the Bible thoroughly. Now, his mind and his ears stood up like the ears of a rabbit. Now, he had to find out what was drawing his keen interest about religion.

His mind snapped back to reality when he heard the noise of the kids and the sound of the front door opening. It was Gloria and the kids returning from the market. He said to himself, I will summon my thoughts of religion later.

The kids and Gloria laughed and giggled to the kitchen. He stood up and stretched his arms over his head and walked toward the kitchen. He had to talk with Gloria and there was no way around it.

The knife landed in his chest with the force of ten 747 jet engines. The knife of reality had hit its target. He was broke; completely impecunious. The house had foreclosed too and his fear now was that Gloria was going to leave him.

His mind began to think of his military training. The military had trained him to deal with any situation and circumstance short of death. He had added to his training the will power to never give up. He had trained his mind to never break under circumstances short of death. The military mind was very difficult to break down and he knew it mind, heart, soul, and body. His ultimate test was at hand though.

The discussion lasted about an hour. It was final. Gloria and the kids were leaving. She was going to live with her parents in Charlotte North Carolina until she found a place for her and the kids. It was the last thing he wanted to hear. nevertheless, the knife of reality had sunken into him like the caving in of a sink hole. There was nothing he could say nor was there anything he could do.

CHAPTER 5
The Test

Two weeks had passed since Gloria and the kids had left. He was all alone now. The days and nights got longer and longer. The drinking had also increased. He was getting drunk more and more. He was depressed about everything and there was seemingly no answer to his ongoing problems. The test was now upon him. The test of his mental capabilities to hang on and deal with his situation until it was all over. And, was he capable of standing up to the test. In his mind he believed in what the military had trained him for. Although, his body and his strength to go on was telling him that he should give up.

He had finished the book called The Christ Commission and had come to the ultimate conclusion in his own mind. There was a God. And, God had a son named Jesus Christ that came to earth and walked among the sinners of the world. Of whom died on a cross for the remission of all the sins of mankind, was raised from the dead three days after his death, and returned to heaven to be with His Father forever. Therefore, he believed in the Holy Trinity and that was final. His question now was, why was all these troubles falling upon him? Why? He knew he himself had no answer nor did he know anybody that did.

The calls were frequent to Gloria. The conversations went on and on and on; seemingly to no end. She was not giving in to coming back. Therefore, he continued to drink more and more and more.

The test was taking a toll on him and he knew it. His mind was thinking more and more. Frustration was taking a hold of him also. He begins to wonder how much longer he could hold on. He knew in his mind that it was all just a test. His question was, was it a test of his mental ability to take on problems or was it a test of his faith? Either way, he had to find a solution.

The two policemen rode in the same squad car. Officer James Marshel and Officer Bobby Hooks of the Gastonia North Carolina police department was on patrol when the call came through. Officer Marshel was a tall black man at about six foot three inches tall with a clean shaved head. Officer Hooks was of average height at five foot 10 inches, Caucasian (white), and had a slightly over sized stomach. They had been on the Gastonia police force for fifteen years among them. Officer Marshel was senior by six months or so. They got along very well with each other. Although, their personal lives were completely opposite of each other. Officer Marshel had a wife and three children. Officer Hooks had a girlfriend and a son by his ex-wife. His son lived with him and his girlfriend. The two of them was loyal to the police force. They both was good policeman. They were also good to the communities they patrolled. Hooks and Marshel was well known by just about everyone in most of the communities in Gastonia. They knew Eight-n-Nine very well too.

Eight-n-Nine was busy finding items (as he called them). He worked himself around town. He would go through neighborhoods here and there, construction sites, and behind convenience stores. Scrap metal and items was his gold mine. Eight-n-Nine had found his place in life and selling items was the epitome of life to him.

He stopped at a Circle K convenience store to grab a cup of coffee. It was early morning. 9:20 a.m. or so on this particular Saturday morning. He got out of his truck and it hit him suddenly that he had to relieve himself. He decided to go to the side of the store where the dumpster was to urinate. He walked toward the side of the building. He always looked down at the ground at stores of this nature (you never know what someone has dropped). As he turned the corner and went toward the back of the dumpster, he saw two black leather shoes sticking out from the side of the dumpster. He slowly walked toward the shoes with caution. He looked down at what the shoes was attached to and could not believe what his eyes was viewing. He gasped for air a time or two with fear and amazement. The words came from his mouth like a soft whisper. He said to himself, Mr. Moses.

He put his right hand over his mouth for what was before him. He could not believe his own eyes. Mr. Moses was stretched out behind the dumpster. He quickly pulled his cell phone from the right front pocket of his Levi blue jeans and dialed 911.

Eight-n-Nine could barely get the conversation finished. He was mumbling his words to the operator. He finally calmed himself enough for the operator to understand what he was telling her. She told him to stay calm until the police got there. He said, Okay and hit the end button on his phone. He put his phone nervously back into his pocket. He knew of no one else he should call.

The police sirens blared at a deafening sound as they approached. The lights continued to flash bright blue as two policemen exited their car. They approached with caution. Eight-n-Nine waved them toward him with quick motions of his hand. He said, Hurry, it is Mr. Moses. Officer Marshel and Officer Hooks looked at each other. Officer Marshel said to his partner, who in the hell is Mr. Moses? Officer Hooks raised his shoulders as to say, I do not know. The two officers leaned over Mr. Moses to see if he was dead or alive. Officer Marshel knelled down and nudged the man on the ground in the side. The man grunted loudly from the nudge of the night stick in his side. He was alive and that brought a sigh of relief to Eight-n-Nine as he nervously looks around the two officers. Officer Hooks spoke first. He said to Mr. Moses, are you alright? He continued on with questions. What is your name sir? Do you have any identification? Mr.

Moses slowly came to his senses. He looked up at the two officers with his right hand shielding his eyes and begin to talk. Before he said anything he could see Eight-n-Nine standing behind the two policemen (seemingly in shock). He said, my name is Eugene Moses. I live just down the road in the Huntington Forest neighborhood. He said, I am a Mechanical Engineer for Myers Mechanical Inc. of Charlotte North Carolina. We make machines for hospitals. I have my identification in my wallet. Eugene reached for his wallet and retrieved his driver's license. He reached his license to officer Marshel. Officer Marshel looked at the license and passed it to officer Hooks. Officer Hooks looked at the license and passed it back to Mr. Moses. Eugene stood up and brushed himself off and begin to explain his reason for falling asleep behind a convenience store dumpster.

His story was that he had a black-out (a state when a person forgets everything during the consumption of alcoholic beverages). After about fifteen minutes of explaining his predicament, Eugene Moses was in the back seat of the squad car and on his way to Gaston Memorial Hospital in Gastonia North Carolina. The two officers decided to admit Mr. Moses for detoxification. Eugene gave no resistance.

Eugene had told the officers about everything; even his wife and children. He told them also about the night before. He had gone to Harrah's Casino with some friends and that was the last of the night he could remember. It all unfolded in bits and pieces in his mind now. He was focused now while in the police car and he could not remember much of anything that had happened last night; almost nothing. He waved at Eight-n-Nine as the squad car rolled out of the parking lot of the convenience store.

The ward was cold. Eugene had found himself on a psychiatric ward. At first it did not trouble him. The days just came and went. He talked to very few people. He stayed alone and to himself mostly. He did not want to make friends with these types of people. He was one of these people now and somehow, he had to cope with it; if he could. He ate some Graham crackers and drank on some milk as he watched the Price IS Right on the television before him. He begins to think sharply now. His mind went back to religion and the test. He now knew that it was all a test of his faith. He could not stop thinking about religion, Gloria, and the kids. In his mind the question came to him like a little child would come to an adult asking for something. Was God trying to get his attention? Was this the test of all test? When and how would he know ran rampant through his mind. He knew within himself that he was not going crazy. He knew too that more answers had to form than the numerous questions now dancing around in his head.

He had talked with numerous doctors and nurses the last six weeks. He knew he was ready to leave. He had to leave or fall in love with one of the nurses. Her name was Bridges Hamilton. She was beautiful. She had long black hair, brown eyes, and very light skin. She liked him and he knew it. She often talked to him when the day room was near empty. Also, she often spoke to him about Jesus Christ. He liked her too, because she did not seem to try to force religion upon him. She just talked to him the way he liked a woman to talk; strong and not forceful. He really could not believe she liked him. He knew he was in pretty bad shape when he got there. Nevertheless, she never hesitated to try to start a conversation with him from the beginning. Therefore, he did not completely fight the temptation. He liked her more and more each time they talked.

Eugene was finally released. Seven weeks had passed and he thanked The Lord that he had made it out of such a place. He knew he had to start all over. He had moved in with his parents. His belongings were at a storage bin. He still had his car (2005 Jaguar) though and that was a plus; the only plus he could remember for a long time now. His car was at his parents' place. He called his mother to pick him up. His moma (as he called her) picked him up about thirty minutes later and he was on his way again. He talked about various subjects surrounding his life with his moma until they got back to Kings Mountain North Carolina. His parents were very concerned for him and he knew it. Nevertheless, there was just nothing he could do about his situation right now. Time was all he had right now and he knew he had to use it well. He had lost everything except his life; everything. His career, his family, and his home. He was at the cusp of losing his mind. His military mind was all he had to work with. He knew from pure experience that the military mind was difficult to break. He had been trained by the best military in the world to cope with anything short of death. He knew he had that to work with at least.

As he drove toward Gastonia North Carolina his thoughts took control. The feeling he had before and during the yard sale had come over him again. It was the trunk. He had opened it weeks ago and found a scroll among other miscellaneous items. The scroll in the trunk came into his thoughts. His belongings were at a storage building in Gastonia. He would go there first. His mind was suddenly at ease. He drove on in complete silence.

The gate to the storage building was closed as he anticipated. He drove up to the code box and entered a few numbers. The gate began to slide open. He slowly drove through the gate and on to the bin that held his belongings. 203 was his bin. He stopped in front of the bin. He got out and stretched his arms toward the sky. He was tired. The last few months had just totally exhausted him. He would get a hotel later and rest. He took the key for the lock on the bin and opened it. The door came up and there it was. The trunk was sitting as he had left it; in the right corner of the bin. It was up front. He pulled it out from the wall and eased the top open. He saw it immediately. The scroll was in plain view. He reached in the trunk and gently removed the scroll. He untied the string surrounding it and begin to unroll the age worn scroll. He begins to read it. His eyes became bulged as he read. He could not fathom what he was now reading. He quickly closed the trunk and set down upon it. He continued to read the scroll.

CHAPTER 6
Pure Love

He called Gloria to plead with her. He talked to the kids also. He told her he was sorry for what had happened to them and he wanted them back. Gloria was always cold to him when they talked. She would tell him, give it time. She loved him and she could not deny it; so much had happened. She had no doubt that Eugene loved her and the kids. It was just pure love between them all. That she was sure of. She knew also, that she could not give in too soon. She was afraid and there was no denying that too. She only could feel sorrow for Eugene and it hurt. Her feelings were in a deep well without light. She only hoped by the grace of God that light would shine again upon their circumstance. Hope was all she had left. She ran everything through her mind at once. The signs were so clear. How could she have prevented all this from happening? She prayed often. She was his and there was no way around it. She would stick with him through it all. Even unto death. Her feelings for him were just that strong. She loved him and that was just that. The memories of the warm sensation in her heart when they kissed was stupendous and she would never forget them.

The calls never ended and they talked longer and longer each time. His family meant the world to him. There was no mistaking that. He had to get them back at nearly any cost. His thoughts raced back and forth like a table tennis match. He could only settle on how much he really loved his family; to a tremendous degree.

He told her about all the substance abuse classes he had taken and the new friends he had acquired. He was making progress. Although, the progress was moving along slowly. He was hurting for his family. Nothing could replace that.

Eight-n-Nine could not get Mr. Moses off his mind as he drove around in his regular neighborhoods looking for scrap metal and items he could sell. He was happy about the way his life was going. Sometimes, he wanted to stop his truck in the middle of the road and get out and leap for joy. Everything was going his way and he was elated about it all. His parents, Betty and Robert took very good care of him. He was thankful for them. The forces above were looking down in good favor toward him. He could feel it often.

His thoughts suddenly shifted back to Mr. Moses.

He could not shake the memory of finding him behind that dumpster. His thoughts continued. Was Mr. Moses alright? Where was his family? And most of all, where was he? He had to answer these questions for himself and that he was sure of. He would try to find out what happened to Mr. Moses.

The fifteen-minute break was almost over. Bridges Hamilton was on break in the day room at the hospital where she had worked for the last twenty years. She had Mr. Moses on her mind and the thoughts would not leave. She truly liked him. She was single and had no children. She had never been married either. A relationship here and there was all she could accomplish. She got lonely more often now and she knew she had to find a man soon. It was just nature. Sex and love were a must have for a woman. There was no way around it. She wanted something more stable now. She was forty-two years old. She could only think of Mr. Moses and how good looking he was when he was there at the hospital. She went back to work.

The hotel room was quiet. Eugene looked around the room. A king-sized bed, a dark brown night stand, a matching dresser, lamps, and a small refrigerator occupied the room with splendor. He begins to think about Bridges Hamilton. The woman at the hospital. He had got to know her well when he was at the hospital. She was gorgeous and single. A perfect match for him. The current situation with Gloria was not going well. He was vulnerable and was well aware of it. He was at an age now when some things just stood out like a swollen finger. His vulnerable feelings for love and comfort were now standing out. He remembered everything about her. He picked up his cell phone and googled the hospital. Hopefully, she was at work today. The phone rang and rung. The automation machine answered and he pressed the number two. She came on the line with a soft hello. He told her who he was and eventually asked her out for dinner. She happily accepted his offer. He closed his phone and leaned his head back against the chair he was sitting in. He was smiling and said to himself, Okay.

The dinner was nice. Steak was the main course (Rib eye). He had green beans, a salad, and mashed potatoes with brown gravy. She had the same. They talked happily among themselves. He asked about her likes and dislikes. He could hear her clearly over the noise of the steak house. She wanted to go out again soon. The hour went by fast. He took her home and returned to the hotel room. No kiss and no sex. Just a friendly hug and goodbye. His mind was fixed on Gloria now and the kids. There was not anything going to interfere with his pure love for his family; anything.

He set down in the chair beside the bed. He reached for the scroll laying on the bed. He continued to read it in its entirety.

He fell asleep after reading the scroll. He woke up in a hot sweat. The dream had seemed so real. He had dreamed of Gloria. They were together again and they were laughing. The kids were laughing too. He could not understand the dream. He grabbed a face cloth and wiped the sweat from his forehead and went back to sleep.

The next morning, he thought more and more about the dream over coffee. What was such a dream telling him and why now? Was God speaking to him again or was it just a coincidence? And why was religion on his mind so much lately? Even though he had gone out with Bridges, his feelings for Gloria never wavered. He was in love with his wife and there was going to be no falling out of love with her; period.

Eugene called Bridges and told her about his situation. She said, I understand. They talked a little while longer and said their goodbyes. Both phones went silent. After hanging up, he said to himself, there is no way I could do this to Gloria.

He called Gloria before she went to work. She was a receptionist for a car dealership. She had worked there for over eighteen years. They conversed back and forth about their predicament. Furthermore, He told her about the scroll he had found in the trunk. He told her about the mind-blowing contents of it. She was taken aback and wanted to see it. He concurred with her request. He suddenly thought to himself- this could be his break with Gloria. They exchanged I love you and hung up.

Eugene put the scroll back on the bed and got dressed for the day. After a long soothing shower, he came out and set down at the dresser. He rushed his hands through his hair as a sign of frustration. He sighed, put on his socks and shoes. He said to himself, I am ready for whatever this day brings. He left the room and headed for the hotel weight room. He was in thought as he walked, he knew he had to keep up his strength and stay conditioned to weather this storm. Also, he knew in his heart he wanted his family back- he missed them so much.

The scroll had changed his thinking forever. As he worked out, a plethora of thoughts cascaded upon his mind. First, he had to find work again. Second, he had to get his family back and third, apply the contents of the scroll to his life. Life to him was like a beautiful flower. It will only stay beautiful for a little while. Eventually, it withers and the beauty is gone forever. Therefore, time was his best friend. He could use it wisely or waste it away. Even so, he knew he did not have time to waste; none. He would go back to the room and look for work on his lap top computer. He pondered his plight a thousand times. He thought through his situation over and over until he was overcome by sleep. His cell phone woke him up. It was Gloria.

CHAPTER 7
The Wise One

The letter was wrapped inside of the scroll. It had been hand written. Signed; Bartholomew Olsen. It read as such: My name is Bartholomew. I am a man of eighty-eight years old. Do not try to locate me. I will be long gone by the time you find me. My days on earth have been many and I know I do not have many left. Attached with this letter is a scroll. Read it in its entirety. Again, read it in its entirety. This scroll has been handed down through my family for hundreds of years. It contains a method of how to live on earth that you should not refuse. Also, it contains a path that you must follow in order to survive. There are many ways to live and there are many ways to die. Your longevity depends on how well you absorb the scroll. It is the only one of its kind left in the world. It was written by my ancestors many years ago. I have not witnessed nor saw any other document of its kind. I lie not. It is no coincidence that you are reading this letter. It was written just for you. I have lived upon earth as a human being for one purpose and one purpose only; to guide you to freedom. I came up poor in the mountains of Asheville North Carolina. My heritage is Cherokee Indian. I converted to Christianity many years ago. I was an electrician for many years of my life. I was once married and fathered two boys. They're all dead now. I am the lone survivor of my entire family history. They lived and they died. You will live and you will die also. It must come upon everything living. The old has to die in order to make room for the new. There is no other way that life works to my knowledge. Take heed that you cherish the scroll. It is your path to where I am going. Therefore, beware of everything around you at all times. Awareness leads to longevity. Watch your steps through life that you fall not into temptation and control your finances. You have no one in your time of need, except the Lord Jesus Christ. Love not money and materialistic things, because they all are only temporary. Your soul and the souls of your loved ones may one day live forever. Therefore, cherish your life and every breath you take. You were planted in the earth by forces beyond earth of which we as humans cannot see. You and I fight a battle between good and evil forces that we have not much knowledge of. I have chosen to fight for the good of existence. My hope is that you will join me in this fight. We do not know for sure of whom created us. We can only be led by our gut instincts and from what we learn. Nevertheless, one day we will be no more on the earth and must continue in another form. Thus, live your life to its greatest heights. Achieve whatsoever your heart desires and take nothing for granted. It is your life. It was given only to you. Live it for yourself and no one else. God intended for you to lead by example and to bring home a good report. It is all left up to you now. It is your duty as a man to leave earth with a good report. The last state of a man is his/her ultimate testimony; whether his/her life was lived good or bad. Your legacy depends on where you go with your life from here. It is vital that you take heed to what I have written to you. It is your choice. No one truly knows when the world will end. All I know is that nothing can begin without an end. Existence was put in place and surly there must be an end. Think about what I have revealed to you. Again, think about all you have read here. I have to go now. Take this letter and the scroll and hug them to your chest. They are all the resources you will need to complete your journey on earth. Go now and do what must be done. Follow the light until it turns dark. Farewell my friend; farewell. Finally, pass the letter and the scroll on when it is time. You will know when the time comes. Signed: Bartholomew Olsen.

CHAPTER 8
The Last Scroll

The scroll read as such: Title, The Last Scroll. Number 1- Love, acknowledge, and believe in God always. Believe in all of His host also, Jesus Christ, The Holy Ghost, and The Holy Angles. They will help you stabilize your life while on earth. Number 2- Remember The Holy Ghost always, because it is your only comforter on earth during the absence of Jesus Christ. Number 3- Respect your family and love them, because in your time of need there is no one else on earth to help you. Number 4- Love not money, because it cannot take another breath for you. You live by the power of God and His host. Number 5- Maintain a good life. Stay focused always and be aware of the evil that can invade your life. Remember, we are fighting a battle between good and evil that we have not much knowledge of. Number 6- Control your own finances, because no one knows what you are in need of more than yourself. Number 7- Keep Sunday Holy unto yourself, because it is your duty as a man/woman to respect God and His host. Number 8- Put away those evil things in your life that blocks your love with Jesus Christ. Do your very best to make the next right decision. Live your life as free as possible without stumbling. Number 9- Stay focused in your mind, because there are evil people among you and around you. Most of the time it is the close ones to you that harbor the most evil toward you. Jealousy can kill your dreams. Stay away from these types of people. Number 10- Judge no one, because you nor I created sin. Therefore, you cannot judge others when you have committed sins yourself. You are just as guilty. Number 11- Stay sober, because the evil one (The Devil) can quickly enter your mind. Number 12- Stay humble always, because you are on earth to represent God and His host. The End. There are only twelve notes here. Each one represents a tribe of Israel. Israel, God's chosen people. Take these twelve notes for your life and keep them near and dear to your heart. They will keep you safe from The Evil One. Farewell my friend, farewell. Signed: Author unknown.

CHAPTER 9
The Reunion

The scroll told Eugene everything he needed to know in order to begin a new way of living and he was not going to pass it up. He had a new opportunity and he was determined to take it. He would eventually regain everything he had lost and more. He was reunited with his family, found another job as a Mechanical Engineer (making six figures), and bought another house in Gastonia, North Carolina.

There was a knock on the door of their new home, the doorbell rang also. Eugene knew instantly of whom it might be. He rushed to the door. Sure enough, it was Eight-n-Nine. He opened the door to a smiling Eight-n-Nine. Eight-n-Nine said, Hey Mr. Moses! How you been, I have been looking all over town for you. Eugene said, how did you find me Eight-n-Nine. Eight-n-Nine said,

Mrs. Madlin told me where you moved to; you know she knows about everything that happens in Gastonia. Eugene laughed and said, yea, you are right Eight-n-Nine. He asked Eight-n-Nine what he had to sell and Eight-n-Nine said, I got a new coffee pot for you Mr. Moses if you need one. Eugene motioned for Eight-n-Nine to come on in the house. Once Eight-n-Nine was inside with the coffee pot. Eugene said, how much do you want for the coffee pot? Eight-n-Nine said, you know me Mr. Moses, if I know you it is eight dollars and if I do not know you it is nine dollars. They both laughed. Eugene said, what the heck Eight-n-Nine I will give you nine dollars for it. Eight-n-Nine said, my man!

After reaching in his right front blue jeans pocket and retrieving nine dollars for Eight-n-Nine. He started to reflect on the recent past. This was a reunion. His family and Eight-n-Nine. Therefore, there was something that needed to be celebrated. It came to his mind instantaneously. They were going to the beach on Friday. Why not invite Eight-n-Nine to go with them to Myrtle Beach South Carolina? Eugene asked Eight-n-Nine if he could go with them and Eight-n-Nine gladly said, yes.

CHAPTER 10
The Author Talks

I brought forth the short story above to illustrate how good and evil can interact in the life of a person. I am fifty-four years old. All my life thus far I have knowledge of existence through the Holy Bible. There is only one other book I have read that shewed light on a question among many in my head. The Christ Commission by Og Mandino shewed a bright light. Again, the question among many is. Did Jesus Christ come to earth as a man? Was Jesus Christ the Savior of the world? After reading the Bible completely through twice and reading the Christ Commission. My answer to the questions above and many others is; Yes. I believe the Bible was manifested through man by God himself. Because, I do not believe that the intelligence of mankind could reach the level of intelligence that is demonstrated throughout the Bible. There is no way man by himself could have written such complicated text as is written in the Bible. See, at this day in time, a majority of the population of the world do not know what their dealing with when it comes to the Bible and Christianity. It is far more complicated than just dressing up in a suit and attending church on Sunday. I believe that there is "something" out there beyond the atmosphere of earth that we as humans lack the knowledge and imagination to know what it could possibly be. Our minds were not designed to fathom this type of understanding. See, "something" (God) put earth in place for His purpose and no one as human should question His reason. I have learned to Pray. I Pray because I and you need some type of connection with the supernatural. We as humans do not know for sure what/who put earth and its inhabitants in place as we know them. I am just saying, beware of what you worship.

I believe in the Divine forces of God, Jesus Christ, and The Holy Ghost. What you believe in is totally up to you. I just know that I have no other concrete knowledge of existence other than that described in The Holy Bible and from reading the book called The Christ Commission by Og Mandino. I am just trying to give you some concrete knowledge here. I am not a preacher. I am just as human as you. Although, I have and have had questions about our existence surface in my mind also. I do not know for sure where I will go when my days be ended on the earth. Again, I do not know where my spirit and soul will rest when this life is over. I do know I will not end up in hell if I chose to believe in Jesus Christ. The above is just my beliefs. Furthermore, I have to believe that there is truth to what is mentioned throughout the Bible. Because I know I did not create a dog, pig, cow, nor horse. Therefore, I know I am dealing with "something" beyond my knowledge and understanding. I do not believe in The Big Bang Theory. I just do not believe an explosion that powerful could have created the universe and its surroundings. There is just no way (to me) that an explosion could have placed earth and the planets surrounding it in such a majestic setting. To my knowledge and understanding, no explosion could ever be that powerful enough to create life as we (humans) know it. Therefore, beware of what you allow your mind to absorb. People are just out to get money at this day in time and they will tell you just about anything. Again, it is not about your wellbeing anymore; it is about that green dollar bill. See, some people could care less about you and your soul. As long as they can get in your pocket, then they are happy. Again, these type people care nothing about you. I care for your wellbeing. I lie not. I care about your spirit and soul; like no other on earth. Therefore, it is the reason I tell you the great things above. Again, I am not a preacher. I claim to be more of a teacher in my writings to you. And as a teacher, I will never try to steer you in the wrong direction.

I look at all the troubles in the school yards. I just believe it all started when the school officials took The Ten Commandments out of the schools and stopped praying. The mass killings of lately at schools is just a warning from God. I just believe that. I just hope the school officials will eventually acknowledge the above and return to normal school routines. I remember it all well, in my days of school (60's-80's) there was no mass shootings at the level we have today. It was virtually unheard of. The only violence was a fight during break; that was about it. The teacher broke it up and that was the end of it. What is going on now is just beyond me.

A plethora of thoughts run through my mind and the above has had me puzzled. I hope and pray that the situation gets better. That is all I can do.

The things I tell you are true. The above was a good example of what is happening today. That is why I say, pray often. Prayer keeps the evil one (the devil) from taking full control of your life. Again, Pray often.

Believe me or not, there is a devil. See, the Bible speaks of the devil. I say again, we as humans are here on earth to fight a battle going on between spirits and forces that we really do not know about. Our minds and imaginations are not strong enough to understand fully as to what is really going on around us that we cannot see. I truly believe that these forces and powers are real. Look at it, can you imagine how chaotic the world would be if there were no supernatural forces controlling it. Therefore, stay in reality. Believe what is simply true and deny those things that are simply false. That is what I call, living in plain ole reality. Furthermore, most things are put in place for a specific reason. Think about it, what would society be like without policemen, doctors, firemen, nurses, and the justice system? And, what would the plants and animals do without rain? And, what would you do without food or shelter? I am just saying, really take a good look at what is going on around you. You will perhaps see the reality that I spoke of above. Again, believe me or not, there is "something" out there beyond earth that controls every aspect of existence. "It" controls the waves of the oceans and seas. "It" controls the very atmosphere we see as space. I warn you! do not continue to neglect the presence of the supernatural. Do not let your soul go down to hell because you did not believe or take heed to my writings. I have been many places in America and I have saw a lot of things. I have still come to the same conclusion I came to years ago; there is a God and His heaven is full of His host. Wisdom, Knowledge, and Understanding are patiently waiting for you to call upon them that they may bestow their powers upon you. All you have to do is acknowledge them and accept them. They are ever standing by to help you with whatever situation you come into or have come through. It is your decision from here on as to whom you will serve and acknowledge. I cannot make that decision for you. Even as I did, I came into this world as one and I will leave this world as one; so, will you. Therefore, take advantage of my writings to you while you still have time. Beware, God is always watching you and I. His eyes are ever beholding everything that happens upon the earth.

CHAPTER 11
What the Scriptures Say Not Me

The Scriptures say: From the Authorized King James Version. From ST. MATTHEW chapter 12: 31-37, Wherefore I say unto you, all manner of sin and blasphemy shall be forgiven unto men, but the blasphemy against the Holy Ghost shall not be forgiven unto men. And whosoever speak a word against the Son of man, it shall be forgiven him: but whosoever speak against the Holy Ghost, it shall not be forgiven him, neither in this world, neither in the world to come. Either make the tree good, and his fruit good; or else make the tree corrupt, and his fruit corrupt; for the tree is known by his fruit. O generation of vipers, how can ye, being evil, speak good things? For out of the abundance of the heart the mouth speak. A good man out of the good treasure of the heart bringeth forth good things; and an evil man out of the evil treasure bringeth forth evil things. But I say unto you, that every idle word that men shall speak, they shall give account thereof in the day of judgment. For by thy words thou shall be justified, and by thy words thou shall be condemned.... Those was the words of Jesus Christ Himself; not my words. These be the words of God Himself speaking through ISAIAH. From ISAIAH chapter 43: verse 3- For I am the Lord thy God, the Holy One of Israel, thy Savior; I gave Egypt for thy ransom, Ethiopia and Seba for thee. Verse 10- Ye are my witnesses, saith the Lord, and my servant whom I have chosen; that ye may know and believe me, and understand that I am he; before me there was no God formed, neither shall there be after me. Verse 11- I, even I, am the Lord; and beside me there is no Savior. Verse 12- I have declared, and have saved, and I have shewed, when there was no strange god among you; therefore, ye are my witnesses, saith the Lord, that I am God. Verse13- Yea, before the day was, I am he; and there is none that can deliver out of my hand; I will work, and who shall let it?

From ISAIAH chapter 44: verse 6- Thus saith the Lord the King of Israel, and his redeemer the Lord of hosts; I am the first, and I am the last; and beside me there is no God.

From ISAIAH chapter 45: verses 5-7; I am the Lord, and there is none else, there is no God beside me; I girded thee, though thou hast not known me; that they may know from the rising of the sun, and from the west, that there is none beside me, I am the Lord, and there is none else. I form the light, and create darkness; I make peace, and create evil; I the Lord do all these things.

The above is just a minute portion of a plethora of verses throughout the Bible that show me God has presented Himself to mankind. I do not need much more proof than what is spoken above to believe in God and His hosts. Again, you can believe what you will. I just truly believe that it is God Himself speaking in the book of ISAIAH. Hey! Stop believing the story of man tampering with the Bible. I tell you; I believe it is just a story to get you to not believe in the Lord, God. Again, look around you and accept the reality surrounding you and perhaps you will believe.

CHAPTER 12
Pushing Forward

The Bible is fulfilling itself every day. The recent mass shooting trend is one example. Trends come and go. The cases are stacking up like paper. The latest, a guy walks into a Waffle House restaurant in Texas and kills four people before one of the employee's confronts him and dislodges the gun from him. These types of attacks are becoming more and more frequent. It is like the trend of drive-by shootings that plagued California back in the 90's.

We as a whole nation cannot allow these trends to continue. Pushing forward is the key. Moving in a positive direction can halt these types of trends. Again, pushing forward together. Making tougher laws for gun control is a great start. Appointing descent public officials is another good place to begin. I look at the present trend of police shootings. There have been twenty-five policemen killed in the line of duty. That is staggering. See, evil is lurking at these days in time. It is like people are raising their hand one at a time and saying, I am next; to kill someone or many. It is like, it is taking very little to set off anger in people these days. I say, it is only the crafty work of the devil. Therefore, we must pray. Jesus taught us how to pray in MATTHEW 6: 7-13. From the Authorized King James Version. It reads as such: But when ye pray, use not vain repetitions as the heathen do; for they think that they shall be heard for their much speaking. Be not ye therefore like unto them; for your father know what things ye have need of, before ye ask him. After this manner therefore pray ye; Our Father which art in heaven, Hallowed be thy name, thy kingdom come, thy will be done in earth, as it is in heaven, give us this day our daily bread and forgive us our debts, as we forgive our debtors, and lead us not in to temptation, but deliver us from evil; For thine is the kingdom, and the power, and the glory, forever, Amen.

See, when you pray; things happen. Good things usually happen. Therefore, pray always, it keeps you in contact with Jesus Christ and His host. The devil will swallow you up if you do not pray. I am writing that you may heed my warning. There is not much time left in your life to wait on things to get better. I too, will soon pass away from this life. I am not troubled. I am ready at any time. I just want you to know that I am in your corner as well. I am pulling for you to win. Pushing forward is about praying for your life to get better. I pray often and I know I am not bound by the devil. He has no power over me. I give him credit for nothing. You can have these feelings as well. Just take the time out of your busy day; and just call on God. Jesus is standing with open arms to receive you. Just believe and you will see for yourself the salvation of God.

The Last Scroll was written that you may understand Jesus Christ. That you may know that He came to earth to save you and I. That His time and life on earth was not in vain. That there was a real purpose behind His presence here on earth. He said, he was going to prepare a place for us. I pray always, that this place is heaven; paradise.

CHAPTER 13
Time is moving on

The time is now. The time to make things right with Jesus. See, time is moving on; to somewhere or something. Do you really think earth and this life is all there is to it? I say no, there has got to be something else beyond earth and this life. Look at it, for thousands upon thousands of years man have sought after something. He has conquered and been conquered. Man has ruled and been ruled. It seems to me that man is always searching for something; wanting more. More money, more power, and more respect. It seems as though man is never satisfied. It seems as though no one is ever completely satisfied. I guess, it is just our nature as humans. We do not know when enough is enough. I am guilty too. I look at the world from many view points and the above is just a mystery to me. I do not see where people are going at these days in time. They seem to have no direction to go in. It is like everybody is waiting for someone else to do something. I am not waiting on anyone. I am trying to line my life up with Jesus Christ. He is the only thing that can fill that void in your heart and soul. With Jesus, I can feel satisfied, I can feel free, and I can feel that there is something better after this life. Do you think we live and die and that is it? If you think that way then I suggest you think a little deeper. Let us face the fact, do you think all of the talk about Jesus is for nothing? Do you think the Bible is just another story? Do you think the resurrection is a myth? Do you think the last day is not coming? Hey! Open your mind and heart and perhaps you can see the truths that I speak of above.

I see, a time when there will be no earth and no people upon it. Therefore, use the precious time you have now to make a place for your soul to rest. That place is with Jesus Christ. I am not writing to saturate you with Christianity. I just want you to acknowledge some of the realities that I see. I do not want you left in the dark.

Down through the ages man has lived upon the earth. There have been many great men that have lived. I look at Billy Graham, I believe he was for Jesus until the end of his life. He lived ninety-nine years and a few days. I believe he was put on earth to represent God. I had the pleasure of seeing Mr. Graham in California in 1985. I was amazed. The crowd was enormous and the money that was collected was astonishing. I knew then that he would become a very famous man. Even then, I believed in Jesus Christ. I am still a believer until this day. I believe too, that Mr. Graham was blessed beyond measure. I do not believe he was in it for the money. I have also been blessed to live to see such men as Billy Graham and many others. I believe I have lived in a blessed era. To live in the same time frame as people like president Barack Obama, James Worthy, Larry Byrd, Mohammad Ali, Micheal Jordan, Bill Clinton, Prince, Micheal Jackson, Tiger Woods, and Lebron James has truly been a blessing to me and I am thankful to the Good Master above for letting my life continue to flourish.

We all (people living) have come a long way. As a whole nation of people, we have accomplished great things and along with you we can do even greater things. Believe me or not, the Good will outweigh the Bad in the end. I just believe there are great things awaiting you and I in the future. Therefore, if you feel as though you are not where you want to be in life (flourishing) then hold on a little longer; your break is just around the corner. I strongly believe that while I am a man on earth, it is my duty to walk before God and His heavenly host. I am not trying to tell anyone how to live. I just want to be a light along someone's dark path. My writings are a light unto your path. Time is moving on; I want you to know that you do not have all the time left in your life to decide to change. Time was set in motion by God (or "something") and as far as I know it has not stopped for anyone. I have come from a mighty long way. I remember living in a four-room house; no running water nor a bath room. Today, I own a three-bedroom house with running water and push button toilets. I am just saying, there is no way under the sun that I could have come this far without the Divine intervention of Jesus Christ. His power shows through me as to just how powerful He is. Also, I have been on the bad side of the law. Today, I live on the good side of the law. I am just letting you know that I too have had my share of ups and downs. I have come through a lot; believe me. I had to change. Period. Today, I walk before God the very best I know how. I know not how much time I have left on earth. Although, I have plans to live a long time. Therefore, take heed to my warning; time is moving on. Do not continue to waste your time. Jesus is waiting to hear your voice.

If you are not doing well right now; call on Jesus. He will help you; whether your situation is good or bad. Again, if your situation is not good; then hold on. Again, I say, hold on. Give yourself a little more time. Time can and will heal most things. Like when Dr. Martin Luther King Jr. lived, he stood upright as a true man and peacefully defended the civil rights for himself and others. To this day, I can see the marks he left on the world. He made a difference. You can make a difference also for yourself. Take control of your life right now and watch the change in your life happen before your very eyes. Again, I cannot tell you how to live. I am only trying to guide you in a different and new direction. I am no God. I can only write to you from experience. I have experienced a lot in my fifty-four years of living. I feel as though I am on cruise control for the remainder of my life. And at some point, in your life I would have it that you feel the same as I. I used Dr. King as an example of many that have occurred sense I have been living. There are so many more.

I speak a lot here about Jesus Christ, because the young people of this country (USA) desperately need Jesus or someone to guide them in a positive direction. The latest mass killings at schools in this country (USA) have been carried out by young people; fourteen to twenty-two years old. I saw on the news just days ago where three boys (fifteen to seventeen) killed a woman in cold blood as a robbery attempt. These types of crimes are happening across the nation (USA) right now. There are so many other cases that I wish not to speak of them. I am just giving you a few examples. Hey! No one wins in these types of cases. I feel sorrow for all involved. That is why I am writing to you right now, because you may not be healthy in your mind and just need someone that will talk to you. I tell you; I am here for you. I want better for you. I am on your side (positively). I hope that I can make a difference right now to someone out there. I want to help someone make things right with themselves. To the adults, I say, Hey! Keep an eye on your children. See, the trouble these days is the parents want to be friends with their kids. I will tell you a thousand times; that will not work. I believe when parents begin to be real parents again; the percentage of killings by young people will fall. Again, parents, stop letting your kids run your household! Clean your entire house; whatever it takes. Begin to be the master of your home. Today, there is very little discipline in homes where there are teens. I am just calling it like I see it. I just feel sorrow when I hear of the type of incidents I described above. The numbers are staggering and continuing to rise. That is why I say, time is moving on. One does not have much more time left to change. Look at the school shootings, church killings (killings of people while attending church functions), and just the average case where someone goes off and kills many people and then themselves. These crimes are horrific and seemingly happening every day at this day in time. Therefore, be aware of whom you associate yourself with. Be aware of your surroundings at all times and mind your own business. I hate to say it, people are getting crazy these days and the scary part to all of this is; you really do not know of whom might go off next. When I say go off, I mean someone is not mentally stable. It is true, I see it happening almost every day now. Breaking news. I look at my own up bringing in the 70's and 80's, if I was out after dark, I got a beating. Period. There was no calling DSS (Department of Social Services). You got beat and that was the end of it. There was no talking back to my parents; absolutely none. And there was no going in the bedrooms and locking the doors for hours and hours. I am just saying, parents were real parents in those days and that is what is wrong at this day in time; there seems to be no more real parents. I only hope that things will get better. I will continue to pray that they do.

CHAPTER 14
Play Time Is Over

The time has come for all adults to become real adults. Play time is over. I said the previous, because it is time to stop playing with yourself and God. You know where you are in your life right now. Either you are doing good or bad, or somewhere in between. I have to be real and say, I am doing pretty good right now. I do not know what tomorrow will bring; no one knows. Therefore, I am living for today and today only. I would have it that you get real with yourself. Really, ask yourself how are you doing? If the answer is I am doing good, then all is fine and well. If the answer is I am doing bad, then the first step toward help is already under way. You acknowledged that things are not the best for you right now. You have admitted there is something wrong in your life right now and you need help with fixing it. I tell you; I do not live a perfect life. I have just made some adjustments along the way. And at this point in my life, I believe I can help someone that may not be where they want to be right now. I can only give to you that I have learned for myself. I cannot give you a perfect life. You have to know for yourself when things are better for you. I do not have a magic wand either. I only have the power that is in me from God. Henceforth, I can tell you how things got better for me. I was forced to give up drinking alcohol and doing drugs. I say I was forced, because I had to force myself from within to acknowledge I had a problem. Then I forced myself to solve the problem. The solution was easy. I was in a place where I had to decide to continue living or die. See, you have to know yourself very well in order to make critical decisions for yourself. If you cannot reason with yourself, then other than Jesus Christ who else can you reason with? And if you do not know yourself at this point, then begin to learn to know yourself better. See, I know that if your life is not where you would like for it to be right now, then you are not knowing who you really are. You have to learn to know the true you. I mean, you are the only one that can decide what you want your life to be or become. You have to begin to know what you are capable of achieving to its maximum capacity. Bottom line, it is time to stop belittling yourself. Again, play time is over. It is the right time now for you to start taking your precious life more serious. Give yourself a real chance at succeeding. It is not all about money and shiny things. I believe you and I have been placed here on earth to be beautiful examples of the powerful work of God and His heavenly host. Look at it, why else would He have made you look so beautiful and in His own image. I tell you; people better start to take a closer look at what we are dealing with when it comes down to dealing with God and existence. It is time to get real. I know I did not make a water fall, ocean waves, or colorful flowers. I do know that "something" did make these things though. I often see different wonders of this world and that is why I have stated what I have. Believe me, I am no fool. I believe that "something" put existence into place for a very unique purpose and I believe that "something" to be God. You can believe what you will. I am just saying, come on people; let us get real for once.

CHAPTER 15
Common Sense

We all to a great degree was born with common sense. I know that my statement can be argued. Nevertheless, most can agree that common sense is common among most humans. I said the above to say this, it does not take a rocket scientist to lead a good life. It only takes a made-up mind. Hey! that is not hard to understand. The problem with society today is that most people think and believe that everything has to be complicated. Technology is the reason. Technology has become so high tech that people think that life today is the same way. It is not that way. Look at it this way, a phone is still called a phone, a jail cell is still a jail cell, a sandwich is still a piece of meat between two slices of bread, and orange juice is still made from squeezed oranges. Again, I am just saying, do not make your life complicated. I just keep things simple.

I live a very simple life style. I am fine with a beat-up ford pick-up truck and a pair of jeans or I can be fine with a Jaguar and an expensive suit. I am just saying, do not let materialistic things define who you are or who you ultimately become. The materialistic things will always follow your pride and dignity. Be proud of who you are first and I promise you that the materialistic things will come to you. At this point in time, it is either you keep up with the world or it will go on around you. Change for you must come. Think about it, I am writing this novel in order to prepare you for your exit from this world. I write in order to strengthen you for the next chapter in your life. I have come to an understanding about life, there is a God and all of His ways we as humans will never fully understand. Therefore, take heed to my writings to you.

This novel is written for the purpose of allowing you to have access to eternal life. It is not to scare you; it is to warn you of the things to come. The world is getting old and time is winding down. You can see it all happening before your own eyes. The everyday killings in Charlotte North Carolina are just one example. The shootings at different schools across the nation (USA) of innocent young people. I reside in Gastonia North Carolina and at age fifty-four I have not seen the level of violence as high as it is in this country (USA) thus far in my life time. It is now 2018. The Holy Bible speaks of times just like we are living in today. I am not just dreaming these horrific crimes up in my sleep at night either. Hey! The above is very real and it can happen to you or in the town or city you reside in; it can happen anywhere and to anybody. I tell you, always be aware of your surroundings and be careful of whom you deal with. Everybody with a smile is not as happy inside as they appear to be. And most of all, everybody is not for you; a lot of people are against you. I have experienced firsthand all that I am revealing to you. I just want you to know of these things now. Then, you cannot say later on in your own life that no one told you. Therefore, use the common sense you were born with and watch your surroundings at all times.

The time is now for you to prepare yourself for the future. Erase the chalk board and draw yourself a new life. The past is gone and cannot be fixed. You cannot look back from this point on. Your life is precious and you deserve success. If you believe in Jesus Christ you cannot fail. Seriously, if you take on a spiritually guided mind you will never fail. See, the weak mind will always spring up and identify itself. Again, the recent school shootings and church shootings are perfect examples of weak minds. The young men that have carried out these horrific crimes seemingly had no spiritual backgrounds; at least to my knowledge. The church shootings puzzle me the most. The nine black people killed by a young white guy at a church in Charleston South Carolina and a similar situation in Texas. These types of crimes are just beyond me. They are crimes that cannot be understood. Therefore, refresh your mind if things seem to be out of focus. Take the time to really think about what you are going to do if things are not well for you right now. If only a few moments, think about it first. I am talking to anyone in the state of mind of doing harm to anyone or many people. Please, get help if you know for sure in your heart that things are not going well in your mind. Talk to someone or pray about it first. I am just saying, do not ruin the remainder of your life just to satisfy a selfish feeling you are obsessed with. That feeling of wanting to harm others will only last for a few moments; life in prison or the death penalty is for an entire life time. It is not worth it.

CHAPTER 16
Where to Next

The life we live now is very beautiful and is precious. The greatest question of all for me is; where to next? Where do we go and how do we exist after this life is over? The Bible speaks of eternal life and I truly believe the Bible. I am not a visionary or futuristic teller. I just see a time of happiness after this life. I may be wrong with my beliefs. Nevertheless, I will continue to believe in the words of the Holy Bible and its contents the remainder of my life. I just hope that I do not live an entire life time here on earth and the above be all false. I just do not believe that man has modified the Bible to the point of falsehood. I was raised as a Southern Baptist and know very little about the religious beliefs of other cultures. I have studied many books about other religions and other cultures during my years spent in high school and college. I still to this day have not found a book more concrete than the Holy Bible. I just do not believe that normal humans could have written such brilliant stories that are revealed in the Bible. I just do not believe that man has the level of intelligence to pull off the complex method in which it was written. There had to be some kind of divine intervention in order for it to be completed. Read it for yourself. You will perhaps see that I lie not concerning this book. I have read in it and through it countless time. I know what I am talking about. Also, I do believe there is a heaven and a hell. I do not have to describe everything to you; you can see the facts about it all every day you live. The paint on the wall is clear to see. See, I look at how society (common in the USA) mostly shows Jesus as a good-looking white guy. And if you think about it there is no way Jesus could have been a natural Caucasian man, because it seems to me that the entire Bible is composed of writings that present the presence of the middle East. Yea, Jesus was described to be a Jewish man by birth. That alone to me says, there is no way He could have been Caucasian. I am just saying, watch what you see and hear. Sometimes you have to look at things another way. I am not saying that all white people are trying to mislead you. I am just saying, draw your own conclusion from your own view point. Use your own thoughts sometime. Believe me, you are more brilliant than you think you are sometimes. I tell you, get the maximum efficiency out of your life, because you do not know how much longer you have to live. I had a friend that lived across the street where I reside here in Gastonia North Carolina. His name was Ken. Ken was a truck driver. He was fifty-eight years old. I watched him leave home yesterday (Wed. May 30th, 2018). Evidently, on his way to work. He was killed last night. Apparently, something went wrong with his truck while on the highway. He was checking out the problem and while doing so his truck was struck by another truck and during the chain reaction he was injured. He died on the way to the hospital. Ken was full of life. I remember watching him leave for church nearly every Sunday morning. His spiritual light shined like the sun. He would tell me often that he wanted to sit on the porch like me when he retired. Also, Ken would do almost anything for you if he could. We would often stand at the top of our street at my drive way and talk; mostly about our current president (Trump). We held many conversations about politics. He will be missed by me alone; as well as his family and others. Rest in Peace my brother. Therefore, you cannot count on tomorrow; for it may never come for you. I am just saying, cherish your life right now as you have it. Live for right now; for right now is basically all you have. I just hope and pray that my friend was prepared (spiritually) for his exit from this life.

I was thinking after I heard of his tragic death, was there anything I could have done to help prevent his death? No. Could I have talked to him a little longer or something during some of our conversations? No. There is nothing we can do in nearly all cases to prevent death. I look at it this way, when your time is over here on earth; it is over. When God calls your number for sure, there is nothing anybody can do. End of story. It is just that way. There is no solution. Death will happen and there is no preventing it. Only the power of the deity can prevent death. I will continue to pray that Ken had his soul ready for the next phase of existence. I fully believe he did. Again, I pray that he was ready. And I say to you, be ready. Always have your house (your inner man/woman) in order, because we (the living) never know when the chilly wind of death will blow our way.

I was talking to my step-son (DJ) on the porch earlier today (the same day of the death of my friend Ken, Wed. May 30, 2018) and I told him as I have told him before. You get one shot at life, get the most out of it while you can, because once it is gone, it is gone forever. When it is final and you are pronounced dead. There is no coming back to earth to live again. I am sorry, it just does not work that way. I told him too, that existence was for a purpose. I just do not believe that whomever or whatever put earth in its place did it all for no purpose. I am just saying, I do not believe that trees, flowers, and people exist without an ultimate purpose. A purpose beyond human comprehension. I just do not believe it. There has got to be a purpose behind all things that exist. And I choose God, Jesus Christ, and the Holy Ghost to be my candidates for creating all existence. Again, you can choose who or whom you may. I am just saying, the above is just what I believe.

As this chapter is called Where to Next. It is my question to you as the reader of this novel. Where to Next? Where do you ultimately want your soul to go when this earthly life is over; heaven or hell? Are you ready for the afterlife? Believe me, I am not only speaking to you. I have asked myself these same questions too. Thus, you are not alone. I write what is real to me. I write to you that you may understand that I am in your corner, always. I try to help you get through the rough times you may be having right now in your life. I tell you; you do not have to live through your situation alone; I am here with you and for you if you take heed to my writings. I will always write in order to try to lift you up. Believe me, no one else is going to give you insight about life as I am. I'll never kick you while you are already down. My spirit is filled with excitement about life. I want to get you to this point as well. I believe we can make it to the top of the mountain together. My hand is open to hold yours. Therefore, take your life more serious and never give up on yourself. You are worth saving. I really believe that your life and mine are special to the Creator of all things. Again, I choose to call the Creator of all existence; God Almighty! The Good Master! The Ruler of all living and dead! And Jesus Christ and The Holy Ghost! These names I can always count on to help me through anything. Through all of my ups and my downs. I tell you, the names of God, Jesus Christ, and The Holy Ghost have never failed me in my times of need. Think about it, would you be alive and reading this novel if "Something" has not been with you up to this point? Come on! You have to give me credit for looking at it all this way. I mean, everything you have gone through to get to this point in this novel and in your life has not been by accident. It is not a coincident either. You are right where you are supposed to be at this point in your life. Right here. Therefore, discontinue your thoughts of being ashamed of your present situation. I am telling you, right now you are exactly where you are supposed to be in life. You do not have to stay where you are right now either. See, I believe our lives was planned out long before we got here to earth. And the one thing you can do to change the course of the plan is to change your life through believing in Jesus Christ. I just believe that I am right where I am supposed to be at this point in my life and I am truly happy with my present situation. If you are not happy with your present situation and want better for yourself, then change your situation. Change the way you live. No one is going to change you for you. You must change yourself. It is like, how do you want the last state of your life to be? Do you want to be found dead under a bridge or in a descent household? How you die is not the point I am trying to make here. A person can die many different ways; I know that. What I am saying is, what condition do you want your life in when it ends? And believe me, one day your life must end. Will you be ready spiritually for the next life? It is all written about in the scriptures. How this world started and how it will end. Again, will you be ready?

CHAPTER 17
Stay Humble

The best way for me to cope with this life and the people I come in contact with is to stay humble. See, to stay humble means to never be boastful about anything or toward anybody. Believe me or not, humbleness attracts good energy. Jesus was humble and was filled with good energy. See, I believe God could have appeared on earth in any form. He could have appeared as a giant, weight lifter, or transformer (The huge characters in the transformer movies). Instead, He chose to appear as a humble man. I believe He (God) chose to appear as a man in order to get more respect. He wants the people of earth to respect His power. He did not want everyone to be afraid of His appearance. That is why I stay humble. My fiancée tells me often that it pleases her to know that I am very humble. It makes me happy that someone has noticed my humble spirit.

Therefore, do your best to be humble or stay humble. Your light (The light of your spirit) will shine brighter and brighter. And I believe that God is pleased with a humble person. Look at it this way, what would you gain if you appeared before everybody as a huge monster? Nothing, because you would scare everybody away from you. No one would come near you or around you. I am just saying, be the best person you can to everybody. You will see that you will gain a lot of respect for yourself.

I guess you ask me as to how I stay humble. Well, I try not to worry about everything going on in my life and I am never concerned about everything that happens. I said the above to say this, you cannot worry about your life, because Jesus will take care of you. And, you cannot be concerned about all of the problems of other people. The news is a perfect example. You cannot absorb in your mind everything that happens on the news stations. It will flood your mind with stress. And stress leads to bad health. Therefore, Like the Bible speaks of, (paraphrasing) Do not worry about tomorrow, tomorrow will take care of itself. Beware of the evil of today. The bible also speaks that God already knows what you are in need of before you ask. It says, the birds are taken care of and they do not work. Therefore, will God not take care of you too? He already knows your goings and comings. He knows all of our ups and downs. I tell you; He will be there for you during the worst of times. He will comfort you during the worst moments of your life. I know from pure experience. Trust Him and see the positive results for yourself.

CHAPTER 18
Attachments

The definition of attachments is, the act of attaching or condition of being attached. (from The American Heritage Dictionary of The English Language). To me, attachments are things we desire or things we cannot seem to let go of. I will use my friend Ken as an example. Ken died unexpectedly. His family buried him today (Tuesday, June 5th, 2018). See, to a large degree I was attached to Ken as a friend. I look at it all this way, be careful about being attached to certain things. Some attachments are just not healthy for you. The unexpected passing of my friend took a lot out of me; mentally and physically. Death can take a lot out of you. I love people and when someone I know passes it just deflates me like a balloon going down. There are many different things we get attached to. Gambling, smoking cigarettes, drinking alcoholic beverages, illegal drugs, lusting for women/men, and eating (one thing or another) are at the top of the list. I am no different than you and you are no different than me when it comes to attachments. We as individuals have many different attachments. Some of mine are different from yours and some of yours are different from mine. We all as a human race have something we are attached to or get attached to. It is just a part of life. It is how you deal with your attachments is what will make you or break you. I say, do not get too attached to anything, because like my friend Ken, it hurts too bad once the attachment is gone. Yea, I just have accepted that his death was just the Will of God and I am alright now with that. I can move on with confidence. And there are things we get attached to that is not healthy for us; like the things I mentioned above. These things can do us harm or cause harm to others. Therefore, beware of things you get attached to. People and things can and will hurt you once they are gone out of your life.

I look at it this way, as I mentioned the Will of God just moments ago. It is what sticks in my mind. Look at your life and your past. It was the Will of God that has brought you to this very moment in your life; nothing else. See, I believe everything that has happened in our (yours and mine) life thus far has happened by the Will of God. I believe too that everything that happens on earth is of the Will of God. There is no way around it either. The Plan of God is perfect; with no mistakes. Again, I go back to the death of my friend Ken. It was not by mistake. God knows more than we do. He knows for His purpose, who to bring into this world and who to take out of this world; so the scriptures can and will be fulfilled. Again, God makes no mistakes. Therefore, take life one day at a time. Get the best out of your life while you still have it. Life is very beautiful. Yea, you will go through difficult times and every day will not be easy to get through. Hold on is what I am trying to say to you. And as far as attachments, if you are attached to one or some of those things mentioned above and they are causing a problem in your life, then release yourself from it. Through the power of Jesus Christ, you can release yourself from any attachment. I do not care what the attachment is, you can release yourself from it. I am not perfect either. I struggle with attachments too. I did let go of the alcohol and drugs years ago. I am just trying to make you aware of the dangers of certain attachments. You know as well as I do that everything is not good for you. Again, I am just trying to guide you in a better direction if things for your life are not as well as you would like for them to be. Hey! I acknowledge that we all have problems that we struggle with. We as humans will always have a problem to deal with here and there as time moves on. Again, I am not perfect; I try to watch what I do engage myself in though. I know for sure that alcohol and illegal drugs once caused me a lot of heart aches. I was doing it all to myself though.

See, we can be our own worst enemy. We seem to constantly cause trouble or do harm to ourselves. I tell you; I do not write about things that I have not experienced myself. I write and learn too; I learn things for myself as I write. I just want to give you the best knowledge as to how to navigate your way through this thing on earth called life; that is my quest and my mission. To get you to a better point in your life through my present and past experiences. Like Mr. Moses from the short story earlier in this novel. Mr. Moses had many attachments and those attachments caused him a lot of problems. Your attachments and mine are not much different from Mr. Moses. And see, Mr. Moses released himself from nearly all of his attachments. I am just saying, it can be done. If you are attached to something that is causing you major problems, then release yourself from it. And I know that everything cannot be stopped all at once. Again, I have an attachment or two myself. All I am saying is, watch yourself. And use the wisdom that you have to guide yourself to better living. Mr. Moses released himself from his attachments through belief in Jesus Christ. I believe in Jesus also. I am just saying, try Jesus and see for yourself how things can be better for your life. Also, read the book called The Christ Commission by Og Mandino. It is the best book I ever read besides the bible that corroborated my faith in the deity. I lie not. This book propelled my faith to another dimension; forever.

CHAPTER 19
Better Times

I see better times in the future for you and me. The past is gone and for the most part, it cannot be recaptured. Therefore, keep your head up and move forward with your life. Forget the past mistakes you have made and look forward to better times. Do not continue to waste time dwelling on your past. You have a bright future in front of you; take advantage of it. See, most of our set backs are caused by dwelling on the past. Again, the past is forever gone and there is not much we can do to go back and change it. We must begin to look toward a brighter future. I can see a better financial situation for myself and for you. You have to trust God more and more at this day in time. You have to believe that God is real. I truly believe that most people suffer with different problems because they do not fully trust that God is real. I have been to the mountains and I have been to beaches in different parts of America. I have seen the beauty of the creations of God. I tell you, nobody on earth can create some of the nature scenes I have beheld. Only God could have made some of the things I have seen. And only God could have brought me through some of the rough situations I have found myself in. I am just using myself as an example to let you know that God can get you through virtually anything. I have been on the very bottom of life. I once had no hope of leading a good life. Today I have much hope and is leading a good life. I hope you can turn things around for yourself as well.

    I write to lift up your spirits. My books are written to lift up your soul. I tell you; I have been there and done that. I have been on top and I have been on the bottom during my life thus far. I just hope and pray that you can learn to lead a better life through my writings. The last scroll is written to perhaps guide you to better times. I hope to have helped you by the end of this novel. You are special to me. You are the reason I continue to write. Again, I see better times for you. I speak to those that may or are having hard times in their life. I speak to those that want to lead a better life. And believe me, it can be done. If someone had told me ten years ago that I would be writing my fourth book, I would have told him/her you are crazy. I would have told him/her the same thing again if him/her would have told me I would be buying a house. I am just trying to show you that things can and will turn around. You just got to trust in God. You have to believe that He can pull you through virtually anything.

CHAPTER 20
Temptations

The biggest stumbling block in our life today is temptation. There is a plethora of temptations. See, temptations hold you back from getting to the place in life you want to be. The bad things (Drugs, alcohol, gambling, lust for man/woman, stealing, and robbery) are the primary reasons most people cannot reach their highest potential. Again, I will use myself as an example. I have done all of the above. Like I have said before, I have not always been a good citizen of this country (USA). Temptation will bring you down. I have been tempted to do many things. Temptation is just an evil force that guides you to trouble with the law. Therefore, watch what you lust for. Your lust for something can and will eventually lead to trouble. If you are in trouble now, get out of your current situation and redirect your life. Prison time is not worth giving up your freedom for. Again, I have been there and done that. I enjoy my freedom today. I take nothing for granted. I cherish all that I have and have accomplished. Again, I believe I am doing well. And, that is what I want for you; to do well. I am not a visionary. Although, I can see that you will see better times. You just have to believe me. Your current situation will not last much longer. Your break in life is just around the corner. Hold on and do not give up. If you are on drugs and alcohol; give it up. It is causing you to stay down. Lift yourself up and conquer those demons. Believe me, excessive drinking and doing drugs is evil. It causes too many problems. Step away from things that are causing you problems. You do not have to fight the battle alone either. Get help if you know you need to. Also, you can call on Jesus. He will always be there for you. He has been there for me and He will and can be there for you. Just try Him and see the results for yourself. See, you are not alone, Jesus was tempted by the devil. He rebuked the devil and the devil went away from him. Therefore, you have to trust that Jesus can deliver you from the devil too. It is no mystery. The power of Jesus Christ is stronger than any other forces. Point blank. Period. His power is the greatest known. The name of Jesus Christ is as fresh today as it was over two-thousand years ago. Do you know of anyone else that has been talked about so much and for so long? I tell you; time is based on His name. You cannot deny that. Time is set up by the time of His birth and death. That is reality and not just what I am saying. Again, Jesus can get you through anything. Look at it, you are still alive right now; something has gotten you to this point in your life and I believe that something is Jesus Christ. He is the only one that could have kept you thus far. I know of no other. I tell you, if Christianity is a hoax, then we all are doomed. Our entire lives will have been spent down here on earth for nothing. And I just do not believe that I am spending time alive for nothing. You can believe what you want to. I just know for myself that Buddha cannot save my soul. No disrespect to anyone for what you chooses to believe in. I just know that my heart, mind, and soul will continue to trust in Jesus Christ. Through Jesus, I have conquered the temptations for drugs and alcohol. And I believe drugs and alcohol was my biggest problems. It took so much from me and it kept me from reaching my highest potential on several occasions. They will destroy your chances to reach your highest potential.

CHAPTER 21
Getting Through

One of the most difficult tasks in life, is getting through. Getting through the tough times. I use to be homeless and had nowhere to go. I still trusted in the Will of God and today I am doing well. I had to trust that by the mercy and grace of God I would live to see better days for myself. I believed that my situation would change and it did. I believe that everything we go through is the Will of God. Everything that happens during the course of a day is of the Will of God. His mercy has brought me this far. I have no doubt. Therefore, if you are in a situation (homeless, addicted to drugs and alcohol, having relationship problems, or financial problems) and feel like there is no way out. Look up toward the sky and call on the Lord Jesus. I tell you; Jesus will not give up on you; He will be there for you. Getting through is the key. Summon your will power and move on. You possess the energy to get through virtually anything. You just have to be sure in your mind as to what you want for yourself and your life. I truly believe that a person can go to all the Narcotics and Alcoholic meetings (NA and AA) they want to. The solution will always be in the mind. When you make up your mind with sincerity and believe in your heart that you can quit; then you can quit virtually anything. You have to build confidence within yourself. You have to want to quit for yourself. Period. Nothing nor anyone can make you quit. Also, you must believe that the deity can help you.

I tried to quit alcohol and drugs on my own and was not successful. I had to believe in myself first and then believe in the Will of God. I tell you, when you take a good look at the way life is, you will begin to accept the Will of God. The Will of God must be done. The money, cars, and houses you have, you cannot take with you when the chilly wind of death blows your way. Therefore, I believe that to do God's Will is to believe that His Will is real and accept that His Will must be done. Know too, that the ultimate plan of God cannot be changed. Gathering understanding and knowledge of God's Almighty power is the only way to understand this life. Reading the bible has helped me understand life to a large degree. You do not have to believe me, read it for yourself and you will know that I have spoken the truth. I have not found or read any other book that can explain our existence here on earth. Again, you can believe what you want to. The power of God and His heavenly host can get you through virtually anything. I am a living witness. Look at it, can you explain life and death happening at the same time. One dies and one is born. Look at the oceans and seas, flowers and trees, mountains and forest, the valleys and water falls, and the many different animals that roam the land. Did we as humans create any of the things mentioned above? No. I know I did not create any of the above. I am just trying to get you to see that there is more to just this life. I believe that there is more behind what we physically see. I believe in heaven and hell. I would hate to have lived this life and end up in hell. I try to treat everybody right. And I will always try to stay humble before God and mankind. I do not know of any other way that I want to live here on earth.

CHAPTER 22
Hold Your Head Up High

I am proud of my accomplishments thus far in my life. I just hope that at this point in your life you can feel the same way I do. I have come from a long way. And I believe that I have come this far only by the mercy and grace of God. I know God has kept me and I will never doubt that. I know He has been with me through all of my ups and downs. I tell you, when things do not seem to be going well; hold your head up high and believe that God will come through for you. I cannot explain it any other way. Again, I have been down on the bottom of life (read my other books), I found a way though to keep my head up and continue to trust in God. I am only telling you about what has worked for me. I have believed in the deity many years now. And I will continue to believe that The Messiah has been to earth and died on the cross for the remission of my sins and yours and went back to heaven to be with His Farther (God Himself). Learn about Jesus and you will begin to see a clear path for your life. Again, hold your head up high and be proud of yourself. You are living a good life. I tell you; life is worth living. And it is alright to be proud of your situation, because you deserve to be proud of having come thus far in your life. I write in the dialogue as to how I speak. I may not be correct at how I say things sometimes. I am only trying to draw your attention as to how powerful God's power really is. I just want to lift up your spirit and let you know that you are not alone with your current situation. It is my pleasure to be with you through difficult times. Again, I write mostly to those who may not be doing so well in life. I just know and believe that you or someone else may need help in one area or another in your life and I want to give you a positive outlook for the remainder of your life. I really believe that I have been saved since Sunday, September 1st, 1991. I have had my share of downs since then, I continued to believe in the Word of God though. God pulled me through when I did not know how I would get through. I was going back in my mind and when I went back to some of the rough days I have lived through; I still wonder how I made it through some of those situations. Today, I know that I had to go through those times in order to get to where I am now. Therefore, keep hope in your heart for your situation and believe that the Almighty God of all existence will pull you through. If you cannot meet your bills or have been heartbroken; call on Jesus and I can assure you that your circumstance will get better. I know, because I have tried it many times. Prayer works. Pray the Lord's Prayer and see for yourself.

Giving up is easy to do when there seems to be no way out of a bad situation. Life was not created to be easy to live. See, when Jesus died on the cross for the remission of our sins, we had to suffer something too. I feel as though God said, I gave my only son in order to save mankind from destruction and as long as mankind lives, he will suffer hard times. There will be obstacles (death, bills, health problems, etc...) in our way as long as we live. The key is how we deal with getting over the obstacles. Your mental state will be tested. Your strength and willpower will be tested. I tell you, never give up though. I learned something valuable from a math course while attending college. Nearly every problem has a solution. I came across only one problem out of all the math problems I ever solved that had a zero solution. Therefore, there is a solution to virtually every problem; you just have to find the solution. And the foundation to solving most of your problems begins with Jesus Christ. He is the problem solver. He will not lead you to a wrong answer. He can and will work out all of your problems. You just have to trust in His Holy name.

The Last Scroll was written to give you hope for a better future. I trust that you will take heed to my writings. I have given you the best of the experiences of my life. I only hope to help you elevate your life to new heights. I hope to give you the confidence to carry on and lead a good life. I tell you; you are at a great point in your life; right now. Keep your head up high.

CHAPTER 23
The Going Away

Sunday, June 17th, 2018. My mother (Sallie Ann Ross- McClain) passed away. She left seven sons. I alone, will miss her dearly. The services were stupendous. The outpouring of love and support from family and friends will never be forgotten. Friends and family members flowed to the house where she resided for over a week. I never have seen that many people before. From the moment we announced the passing away of our mother, people flowed back and forth to her house for more than a week. The entire event was overwhelming to me. I was held together by the love and support of the community, friends, and family members. I will never forget the going away ceremony for our mother. Rest in peace moma.

I wrote the above for a purpose. See, as much as

I dislike the passing of our mother. I come to understand that it was the will of God that she departs this life. And my conclusion is such, we all have a going away in the future. There is nothing we can say or do about it. All I know now is that I must prepare myself (my soul) to meet my maker. I spoke earlier about attachments. No one loved my mother as much as I feel as I did. Although, I drew back from that love a few years ago. Lord knows I loved her. Nevertheless, to be able to deal with the passing of a loved one you must learn how to not get too attached to anything here on earth. Materialistic things, loved ones, and people in general are temporal. Nothing on earth will last forever. The key to it all is to get your soul in order to meet The Creator. Again, I choose to call The Creator (God Almighty). This novel is based on the very things mentioned above. I am not a preacher. I consider myself a teacher. See, the spirit is within us and it must leave us one day. One day your life as well as my own will be no more in the earth. If you are not prepared, then start now to get prepared. Your day of death will soon be at hand. I did not write this novel in order to frighten anyone. I am writing this novel as to the facts of reality.

During the process of the going away of my mother. I learned one invaluable thing; save your money. Do not get caught off guard. You will need money for the unexpected. And trust me, the unexpected is going to happen. I had to make several adjustments to my financial structure in order to be alright during the burial process. I tell you, always be prepared for the unexpected. I was not properly prepared for the passing away of my mother. Again, I had to make sudden adjustments and that is not the way life should work; I was caught off guard. I am fine now. Although, I had to sacrifice. What I am saying to you is, get your house in order. Do not let the Lord come as a thief in the night and find that your house (your soul) is not in order. I tell you; death of a family member can alter the way you live. I do not mean the previous in a bad way. I am just saying, death will affect your family in ways you would never have imagined. I know it is a subject that is rarely talked about among family members. Actually, it is rarely talked about at all during events and family gatherings. I am speaking from experience; it is not talked about as much as it needs to be among African- American families. My own included. I talked about it often before the passing away of my mother. And it seemed as though she was not direct with me with the specifics of what was to happen in case of her death. It is sad that the number one event that is surely going to happen, no one wants to talk about it. I am going to talk about it from now on. It is just a situation that can no longer be avoided.

The going away services for my mother was awesome. She lived her life as a born-again Christian. She believed in Jesus Christ. She says, she was saved in 1984. She was seventy- four years of age when she passed away. She had been alcohol free for nearly forty years. She never used (A.A.) Alcoholic Anonymous or (N.A.) Narcotics Anonymous or any other program. She believed in Jesus Christ until she died. The main thing I am trying to tell you is, get yourself ready to depart from earth and this life. Hey! You cannot take anything down here on earth with you either. Therefore, do not get too attached to materialistic things. Cars, houses, jewelry, and fine clothes. It is all temporal. I am not saying that having nice things is wrong. I am simply saying, do not get too attached to materialistic things and the material gain of this world. For it is all going to one day pass away like a day of last week. I tell you, the best thing you can do between now and when you pass away, is get your soul ready to transition to the afterlife. Get your life in order. I have to make some adjustments too. I do know one thing for sure, I will continue to believe in Jesus Christ and the rest of the Heavenly Host until the day of my passing away. I look forward to meeting my maker one day. The going away of my soul will be the greatest event ever I have known. Death can happen at any moment and the best thing a person can do is be ready. As I say, to you, that chilly wind of death will blow your way one day. Will you be ready?

CHAPTER 24
Good and Evil

Good and evil clash all the time. Can you discern good and evil? To discern good and evil is not an easy task. The mind is constantly in motion back and forth trying to separate the two. Therefore, you have to train your mind to choose the good. Training your mind to do the right things is the first step. I mean, when you know for sure what the right thing is, do it. Do the right thing over and over and over until you get used to it. Then, your mind will respond and react to your decisions. See, as a man I know that most of the time grown men do not like to listen to other people. We like to make decisions on our own. And that sometimes is a dangerous thing. I had to make up my own mind when it came to making some of the most important decisions for the remainder of my life. I made serious decisions about how I wanted to carry out my life. Thus far, I have done well. A few years ago, the devil had his evil spirit upon me. I was in Asheville North Carolina in a government program that helps veterans re-establish themselves back into society after drug and alcohol addiction. I got depressed one day and tried to drink a malt liquor beer while on medicines prescribed by the Veterans Administration (V.A.). I became sick almost immediately and developed cramps in my stomach to the point that I thought I was going to die. I was in some woods behind the store where no one could see me. I honestly thought I was going to die. I eventually got better. I have not had another drop of alcohol since. That was in the summer of 2013. Five years ago, I made a decision that stands today. I made the decision to stop drinking and doing illegal drugs for the remainder of my natural life.

I had to practice that decision over and over in my mind until my mind accepted it. I tell you, today it rarely crosses my mind to drink or do drugs. I just simply do not want those things as a part of my life anymore. The devil had his grip on me and it was up to me alone to make the decision that would release me. See, the devil can and will attack you every chance he can get. We as humans cannot comprehend the war going on between GOOD and EVIL as the Bible speaks of. The war is ours as believers in the flesh. Although, the battle is not ours. The war is between spirits of another dimension that we as humans do not have the mental capabilities to comprehend. I do believe that there is such a war. Because, the world around us is often showing the evidence of a clash between good and evil.

Just look at Charlotte North Carolina alone and you will see for yourself that I lie not. I am almost afraid to go to Charlotte North Carolina these days. The city has seemingly become a major killing ground. It is a killing there almost every day now. Do not get me wrong here, Charlotte North Carolina is a beautiful city and there are plenty of good neighborhoods there. I am just saying, there is a lot of evil going on in that city right now.

I believe though, God controls everything; the Good and the Evil. ISAIAH chapter 45, verse 7. Gives me the confidence to carry on with my life regardless of what is going on around me. I believe! Therefore, live out your life the way you see best for yourself. For when the time comes for you to exit this world; only God will make that decision. Again, you brought nothing into this world and surly you will take nothing with you when you die. That is just the way it is. Learn to love your neighbor as you love yourself. Seek peace, joy, and happiness. Respect your elders and help someone when you can. Love for the next woman/man will cover a multitude of sins. I am just saying, keep your mind and heart clean toward others and your life will blossom like the blooms of a flower.

See, we do not control anything as some people may think. The deity runs the whole earth. My brother (Roydell) said it best, God runs the whole world at one time, all the time. The devil cannot enter your life on his own, he must have the commandment from God. That is what prayer is for. To pray that God keeps the evil one from us. I tell you, Good and evil is real. The devil is real and hell is real. Death has been real from the beginning. When Adam ate from the tree of life as spoken of in the Holy Bible, God set death for man into motion and to my knowledge, God has not changed His mind and heart about death since. You must begin to face reality, one day you and I will die. It is the only way to have a chance to get to heaven. I just never would have thought my mother would die so soon. It happened so suddenly. She was here one moment and gone the next moment. A blood clot stopped her heart instantly as explained to us by the medical examiner. Therefore, I learned an invaluable lessen from the sudden death of my mother; stop thinking and assuming that your loved ones are automatically alright. Stop taking life for granted. Learn to check on your loved ones often, because in an instant they can be gone. Again, cherish your loved ones now while you have them here alive. You never know how much you miss someone until they are gone.

CHAPTER 25
Acceptance

The most difficult feeling to cope with from the passing away of my mother is, Acceptance. Accepting reality. I know life must go on. And having accepted now that she is gone. I can move on. I do not know if you have lost one or both parents. I can tell you this, honor your parents always. For when they are gone into the next life, there is no more you can say or do for them. To believe in the deity is what keeps me going. See, you got to trust that God is truly on the throne and there is nothing He will not do for those that love Him. To cope with anything in this life is to believe that God is constantly in control. That He controls the living and the dead. He controls the entire universe. Also, there are no mistakes made by God. His decisions are made with facts and no one on earth can change the course of His plan. When things happen such as death, we just have to adjust the best we know how and move on with our own lives. Would of, could of, and should of means nothing. Therefore, love your loved ones now while the blood is still running warm in their bodies. For when they leave this old world, there will be no more loving to be done. Cope with life with faith and I promise you your life will be better. You just have to focus on what is most important to you. Do not worry about what you do not have; be thankful for the things you already have. Again, you are living better than you think you are. Accepting reality is a constant method for managing one's life. It must be practiced daily in order to maintain a stable life. The ones that fall from the face of reality fall into sinful activities.

    Be who you are and do not worry about others. For ages, people have said, good and bad things. If they talked about Jesus, why would you become exempt from slander and hearsay? No one is perfect in the flesh. We all have made mistakes and done wrong to some degree. The one thing we can do is be faithful toward God. Do what is best for your own life. See, I am not going to steer you in the wrong direction. I am writing to give you a new direction to travel as you finish out your life. I hope that you can change your direction by taking heed to my writings. This entire novel is the last scroll. Believe me, no one else is going to give you insight about life as I am. My experiences thus far in my own life can and will help you redirect your life. My books are designed to lift people up out of despair. My books can help you through virtually any situation. If you are in jail or prison, going through domestic problems, caught up in addiction with illegal drugs and alcohol, and abuse. I can help you. Your life is not over yet and you can turn things around. Again, acceptance is the first step. You must accept that there is a problem existing in your life for which you do not have a quick solution for. Then, you must truly believe in Jesus Christ and believe that He and He alone can help you through your situation. The rest will fix itself. You have to constantly believe in your heart that things can and will get better. Again, I do not have a magic wand. I do not know your circumstance or situation as well as you do. I can only give you hope from my experiences.

The 4th of July, 2018 (American Independence Day) has come and gone. The gathering of family and friends was at our residence here in Gastonia North Carolina. It was a blast. We grilled out chicken, ribs, hot dogs, and fried fish. We played cards and laughed until late evening. There were many people and plenty of food. It was really nice. No arguments and no fighting. Rare with family gatherings. Later that night I and my fiancée went over to my brother's house and his son had fireworks. My brother's son (AJ) had a plethora of fireworks and he had a fabulous time shooting them off. We had a very good time. I had my moments as remembering our late mother. She was the missing piece to a beautiful puzzle of fun time. She loved fireworks and loved to see others have a good time. After the fireworks we returned home and the day was a done deal. I will never forget the fireworks display my nephew (AJ) put on. It was so beautiful! I plan to get some myself next year, if it be the Lords will. I love myself some fire works!

Therefore, learn to enjoy your life. Keep your head up and continue moving forward. Reality is real. You cannot fake reality. Learn to accept reality for what it is worth. Living in reality will give you a peace of mind. You will be at peace with yourself. I have traveled around this country (USA) and I have found that you cannot find peace anywhere on earth until you find peace within yourself. You can travel the world over looking for peace and happiness. You will not find them anywhere, except you look inside yourself. See, you are the most important person in your life. I have found that if you do not care for the way you live your life, then no one else will either.

My mother always wanted her children to become the best human beings known to man. She always encouraged me and my other brothers to do better. Be better tomorrow than you were today. Grow and never give up on ourselves.

The reality today is that parents are letting their children raise them. There is no strict discipline anymore. The parents of today want to be friends with their children, which is a terrible mistake. To guide a child means correcting that child from time to time and letting them know with a degree of fear that you as the parent will run your household. I believe that the young men that have been shooting and killing innocent children in the school system lately, have done those horrific acts simply due to not having been disciplined at home. None of these guys had any ties or connections with the spiritual realm. They stayed isolated. I tell you, if you have a kid or young man living in the same household with you and you allow them to stay isolated in their bedroom without checking to see what they're doing, it is the red flag. I am sorry, something is wrong with that picture. Hey! Check on your child/children. You may just save countless of innocent lives.

Again, Acceptance. Learn to accept reality for the truth that it is. Reality will never be false. You cannot make a train turn into a plane. Accept your situation as it truly is right now (if bad) and figure out a way to make it better. No one will try to lift you up if your plans are to stay down. No one can make you stand up if you do not want to. Plain and simple. Mr. Moses accepted his situation and sought after a solution. He solved the problem; he did not let the problem solve him. Time can work out a multitude of problems also. You have to give yourself some time. Your situation did not become what it is right now overnight. It took time to develop. Now, it will take time to fix the problems surrounding your life. There is no quick fix; in most cases. I found through my experiences that you cannot solve any problem until you accept that in fact a problem exists. Then, seek diligently for a solution.

When I was in active addiction to illegal drugs and excessive use of alcohol. I first had to decide what was more important to me. Continue to destroy my life to the point of death or live. I had to dig to the greatest depths of my soul for an answer. See, when you are caught up into addiction you can become comfortable with living that way. It can become your reason for living.

The problem with some people today is the fact that they have become comfortable with living in addiction. I tell you the truth, you do not have to become comfortable with that type of life. The way out is to become aware of who you really are. The person you are when there are no drugs and alcohol in your system. Again, look at reality. You know you can be a better person and lead a better life. You know deep within yourself a beautiful human being does exist. You possess the will power and the strength to become whatsoever you want to become. It is not too late to follow your dreams of the past and present. You must believe in yourself enough to realize that a change can happen. Again, this entire novel was written to give you a different perspective on life. Again, this is the last scroll. No one is going to give you the truth about life like I am in this novel. Life is so precious. I believe there is a deeper meaning to life than we as humans can imagine. Behold the beauty of earth and beyond and you may perhaps see what I mean. We as humans just did not appear here on earth by accident, nor is our existence a coincidence. I believe there is purpose for everything that exist and that will exist in the future. There is something beyond the sky, moon, sun, and stars. And whatsoever that "something" is, it is powerful. I believe that "something" is God.

Therefore, if you know that you are not saved, get saved while there is still time. I have been saved since September 1st, 1991(Sunday). I was living in the shelter in Charlotte North Carolina. I had been there a day or so. A church bus came and offered people to attend church services that morning. I decided to go. During the service I saw the magnificent glory of God and His heavenly host. I will never forget the scene in that church. I truly believe God showed me the beauty of His glory. A Pastor Gool was preaching. I still believe the church is still established. The awesome beauty of the church inside is what drew my attention. The massive beams in the ceiling and the number of people in attendance was overwhelming to me. My conclusion was that nothing could do such a thing except it be God. I got saved that day after the services and I believe I have been saved since that day.

     I have had my share of ups and downs since then. Although, I have not relinquished my beliefs. That day I began to study the Bible (The Original King James Version) and I have believed in God and all of His heavenly host since. I believe the story of Jesus Christ. I believe that He came to earth and lived a sinless life, died on the cross for the remission of all the sins of mankind, and ascended into heaven to forever be with the Father (God). I believe Jesus rose from the grave after three days and walked among His disciples before ascending into heaven. The Bible says, if you believe in the above, you Shall be saved. I focus and meditate on these beliefs' night and day. You can have peace in your life also. You just have to believe.

CHAPTER 26
Encouragement

Encouragement is one of many words used that is the beginning of movement toward success. Success can come in a multitude of forms. During my days in High School at Kings Mountain Senior High School in Kings Mountain North Carolina. From 1978 to 1981. I had two people that was influential in my life. Mr. Moffitt and Mr. Guy. Mr. Moffitt was the wrestling coach and Mr. Guy was my drafting teacher. They kept me motivated to become the best at whatever I wanted to pursue in life. They were both white and neither one of them was ever racist toward anyone. They always encouraged me the entire time I was in High School. Our wrestling team was composed of mostly African-American boys and Mr. Moffitt treated us all as though we were his children. He was never biased toward us because we were black (African-American).

Mr. Guy was the same as Mr. Moffitt in many ways. Mr. Guy always encouraged me to be the best at drafting (Mechanical Drawings). His influence propelled me and motivated me to go to college. I enrolled into Gaston College in Dallas North Carolina immediately after graduating from High School. I earned my Associates Degree in Mechanical Engineering Technology in 2005. I thank Mr. Moffitt and Mr. Guy for all the encouragement they gave me to this day.

I look again at my brother (Roydell). I encouraged him to turn from a life in the streets. He took my advice and he has been clean and sober for more than twenty-eight years. He has a wife (Karen) and two children (Kendrick and "Punkin") and has worked for the same company for nearly eighteen years. A very beautiful family. Therefore, if you are in active addiction, surround yourself with people that will encourage you to do better for yourself. Get some help. I speak to anyone that is struggling with leading a decent life style. Again, I am not perfect. I just know from my own personal experiences that leading a decent life style does not always have to be a struggle. Life is good, we as people make things seem harder than they really are; in many cases. You just got to choose the direction in which you want your life to go in. The struggle to live a good life is not your problem; you are the problem. I am just speaking the truth. See, a lot of people will try to sugar coat reality for you. I am not that way. I see things from a different perspective. I have probably been in the situation you are in now. I can sympathize to the problems and pain you may be dealing with right now.

The way out of your situation is to believe in the Lord Jesus; first. The rest will work itself out. I promise you. You can overcome virtually any problem by taking heed to my writings.

Think about this, do you want to continue as you are or stop and be better off in the next five years? It is never too late to start over. Begin a new life. I do not know your current situation. If it is not good, then this novel is for you. I write to encourage people to change the direction of their lives. It does not matter what your situation is right now. You can change it. Again, if you are dealing with addiction to illegal drugs and alcohol, Pills, Relationship problems (Abuse), Going through a nasty divorce, Depression, Suicidal, Loneliness, and Helplessness. I tell you; things will get better. Just hold on. It takes time. Time can heal a lot of pain and solve a plethora of problems. Give yourself a chance. I believe in you. You just have to believe in yourself too. I encourage you now, do the next right thing for your life.

CHAPTER 27
Best Chance

I hope you have enjoyed this novel thus far. It has been my pleasure to come before you. I feel that this is my best chance to capture your undivided attention. I have written to you about numerous subjects. I only come to you in this fashion, because I care for you and want the best for you. Again, my brother (Roydell) is a prime example of what my writings are about. I encouraged him one night when he was at his lowest point. His battle with drugs and alcohol was consuming him and his life. He had nowhere to go nor anyone to turn to. I asked him that night to go with me to Charlotte North Carolina to seek help for his hopeless circumstance. I really was in no shape to help anyone clean up their life. I was still in active addition too and I wanted to seek help for both of us. Even though I was not where I wanted to be in life. I could see something in Roydell ("Roy") that he could not see in himself. I saw an upstanding man that was full of compassion and love for others. I knew too that if he cared so much for others, he had to care for himself somewhere deep in his heart and soul. He agreed with my suggestion and followed me to Charlotte. We left walking from Kings Mountain North Carolina. We did not have a clue as to how we would get to Charlotte North Carolina; which was forty or so miles from Kings Mountain North Carolina. We pressed on and finally caught a ride from a friend we grew up with in Ebenezer (A predominately black neighborhood in Kings Mountain North Carolina). We had walked about twenty-five miles before our friend picked us up. It was only the power of God to allow this man to stop on busy highway eighty-five at night to give us a ride. We ended up at a detoxification center and Roy decided to stay. It has been almost twenty-eight years since that night. From that night until this day (July 23rd, 2018), Roy has been clean and sober. Amazing I tell you; he now resides in Asheville North Carolina with his wife (Karen) and two children.

The moral to the magnificent story above is that at any time, anyone can change. The proof is written above. Like I said, this is my best chance and attempt to reach the inner you. Today, I am clean and sober too. I do not take my sobriety for granted. I pray and thank Jesus Christ for every day I do not consume alcohol or illegal drugs. I love the life I live today. I would not want to trade it for all the money in the world. I took my best chance at becoming clean and sober about six years ago. I was determined to quit. I had no choice. I was drinking alcohol while on prescribed medicines. It was either I quit or die; plain and simple. I gladly chose to live a little longer. Sometimes, you will have to make decisions that will affect your entire life. Life is just that way. The situation will help you decide. You just have to make the right choice. After reading the above, what will you decide from here to do with the remainder of your life? Do you want to sink or float? There is nowhere to stand between these two choices.

Again, I have come to you in so many ways. My only hope is that you will take heed to my writings. Take action now, while you still have a chance. I heard my brother (Lance) say, there is a difference between listening and hearing. The difference is that when you hear someone speaking to you, you take no action. When you listen to someone speaking to you, you take action. In other words, you act and do something about your situation or circumstances. I hope that you will take action and begin to live a productive life.

I have likened life to that of a well-prepared meal for Thanksgiving or Christmas. The food is beautiful and delicious. The different conversations going on simultaneously, an atmosphere of laughter, and fun activities for the children. The perfect setting. I look at life with the same since of joy and happiness.

You can do the same with your own life. See, as long as we have breath in our bodies, we have a chance to get things right with God. God knows your heart and the contents therein. He knows our ins and outs, our comings and our goings. You may think it was a mistake that you exist. Let me be the first to tell you, you are not a mistake. Because, the God I serve and the Jesus Christ I believe in; made no mistakes with creation. He (God) created man for His purpose. Neither you nor I know what that purpose was. All I know is what I have read and know within my heart. The knowledge I have acquired has been stupendous. The understanding I have obtained has been incredible. The wisdom bestowed upon me has been unsearchable. He can do the same for you. You just have to accept that the powers of God and His heavenly host are real. As real as knocking on a wooden door. Again, you cannot fake reality. Reality is real and there is no way around it. You cannot make a peach be a banana. You cannot make an apple be an orange. Play the game of life fair and the game of life will be fair to you. You can get through your particular situation or circumstance. You just have to gather yourself and try. Truly trying can solve ninety-five percent of your problems. The other five percent is having faith in God and having the will power to carry on with your life. The rest will fix itself. Choose the right path and the right path will guide you. Let the good in you show outwardly. Let the world around you see the best you. You are vital to existence. The world would not be the same without you. Again, I am in your corner. I want you to lead a spectacular life style. Give yourself an honest chance and you will see the beautiful results for yourself. I took my best chance to lead a better life years ago. Now, you have your best chance. Take that chance. The opportunity to succeed or lead a better life style is before you through my writings. I give you my personal blessings to the crucial decisions you make from here. It is all up to you. Play or be played. You take control of your life or life will take control of you.

CHAPTER 28
Days Ahead

I see better days ahead for you. I have come to you as humble as I know how. I have a vision for the remainder of your life. You will prosper and become a great person. I can see your life shine like the lights along the Las Vegas strip or the glamour of the view of the spectacular lights of the sky-line of New York City. You just have to believe in yourself enough. Again, take heed to my writings. Begin a new life style. It is alright for you to live again. I have given you the best of my own experiences and I hope you will follow my lead.

Again, I can sympathize with you in your current situation or circumstance. I was once lost in this huge world too. Alone (Homeless) and nowhere to go. Nor did I have anyone to turn to. I have had to play the street life (Completely). I have been drunk and on illegal drugs to the point of losing my mind. Therefore, I can relate to virtually any situation you are faced with right now. I tell you; I have been there and done that; countless times. I suggest to you right now, find a way through your situation. You can do it! Stop believing that your life is over at this point. You have time to pull things together. That time is now though. Throughout this novel thus far I have given you some of the best knowledge known to man for living a productive life style. Hey! I would not want to do anything other than what I am doing right now. I would not trade my life style for all the jewels and money in this world. I have accepted reality. The reality that I might not ever become rich or famous. I have accepted that my life is structured to be lived on even playing grounds. I do not expect fame or riches for the remainder of my life. In other words, I now choose to lead a normal life style.

Again, I see the same life style for you. Normal everyday living. I am proud of my progress over the past several years. I take my medicines in the morning and live out the day (Alcohol and drug free). I was discharged from the military under medical conditions in 1986. Today, I am one-hundred percent disabled. I am proud that I served in the United States Military. I have good days and I have bad days. See, I have waited thus far into this novel to reveal the above. I did it on purpose. I just realized that this is the point you needed to know that I too struggle with something. Therefore, you are not alone; Mentally, Spiritually, and physically. Again, I am proud of the progress I have made over the years since leaving the military. Today, I have one son, five grand-children and a fiancée. I love them all to the end of the world and beyond. They all love me too. They all (The grand-children) love to play and have fun. I would not trade them for anything in this world. I now reside in a great neighborhood in Gastonia North Carolina. I plan to marry my fiancée very soon.

I have given you the above of myself. I hope to give you confidence that you too can lead a good and productive life. Believe me, it does not take much. Abide by the law and everything else will fall into place; I promise you. Take command of your life now and look forward to beginning better days of living. Again, if you are in active addiction, please, seek help! Help is out there waiting for you to come and receive it. See, I know that everyone is different and it takes different things to help different people. I am just saying, whatever help you may need is out there and most of all, it is available to you in one form or another. It is 2018, there is no excuse for anyone to suffer from lack of help here in America. I am sorry, I just had to speak what is on my mind and in my heart. Again, there is no excuse! If you want to lead a better life, then do what you got to do. Just keep everything right by the law and you will see better days ahead. It is all simple, just do the next right thing.

CHAPTER 29
Learn to Be Alright

One key to opening the lock that leads to living a good life style is learning to be alright. Being alright with yourself and the life you now lead. Learn to enjoy the many freedoms of living in America. You can live anywhere and be happy within that particular environment. The town, city, or country you live is not what is keeping you from leading a better life. You have to learn to be comfortable with yourself first and then, happiness will follow. See, I use to think I would be addicted to drugs and alcohol all my life. I once got comfortable with being drunk and spending all of my money. Along the way though, I made some critical decisions about my life. I got serious with myself. I had to learn to understand myself within. I said to myself, I do not want to spend another day of my life like this. I got completely feed up with having black-outs, vomiting in toilets, and getting in trouble with the law. I was sick of it all. The running around in the street's night and day, dealing with people I did not know, and sleeping in strange places. A nightmare I tell you. I always had hope though and I never lost focus of leading a better life. I commend myself for going to college too. Because, even though I was once fully engulfed in consuming alcohol and drugs; I always stored in the back of my mind that I would one day lead a productive life. I never indulged in drugs to the point of being a full-blown addict. Alcohol was my drug of choice. Today, I am living a productive life. Again, I am not perfect and I do not live a perfect life style. I just try to do the next right thing.

In other words, I try to stay in my own lane. Life seems to work better for me that way. Learn to be alright and stay in your lane. I tell you; you know deep within your heart and soul the kind of life you want to live. I am not telling you what you must do with your life. I write to you from the deepest depths of my mind and heart. I can only tell you about my experiences thus far and what I did to get me where I am now. I am trying to be a positive example to you and others. See, there are numerous people in trouble in one form or another. I hope to reach anyone that may be in a crisis and want help. I cannot point my finger at anyone and say, you need to quit doing this or that. Because, I have done some wrong in my life too. The Bible says, we all have sinned and come short of the glory of God (Paraphrased). Therefore, how can I bash you for your sins when I have sinned too. It is like, cut up the fallen tree in your own yard before you complain about the fallen tree in my yard. I am just saying, people always want to point the finger at others and overlook the wrong that they do. You know what I mean. I am sure you can attest to the above.

Also, praying will help you learn to be alright. I have mentioned God and Jesus Christ many times throughout this novel. I use only what I have learned in order to carry out my day-to-day activities. Prayer helps me to focus on what I need to do next in order to lead a positive life style. Prayer will give you a personal connection with the unseen forces. I believe every living soul on earth today believes in God. Countless of people try to worship the forces in many different forms. Although, many try to deny the presence of a specific Ruler of All Creation. For me, I will choose to call my Lord and Savior, Jesus Christ; God being the Father of all Creation. And the Holy Ghost being the spiritual Comforter on earth. I just believe we all as a human race believes in "Something" and I choose to call that "Something" (God). You can choose whomever you like. If worshiping a six-foot-tall carrot is your preference, then so be it. I tell you though, in whom will you call on in your time of troubles. You better hope that six-foot carrot can pull you through. Again, I have had some pretty rough times in the past and I always trusted Jesus Christ to pull me through. I cannot think of any time that Jesus did not come through for me. I do not believe that anyone can calm a storm like Jesus. I just turned fifty-five years old about a month or so ago and in all my years of living thus far, I have not seen anything come close to matching the power, grace, and mercy of Jesus Christ. He has brought me to where I am now. I would not trust any other powers.

I hope you have enjoyed reading this novel. Again, it has been my pleasure. I have given you some of my best knowledge about life. The ultimate decision is now in your hands. Do what you feel you must do to be alright. When I say, learn to be alright, I mean, take control of your present situation or circumstance and turn your life around. It is alright to own or have houses, boats, cars, and loved ones (a nice family). You can enjoy whatsoever you want to buy. Happiness is yours too. You can be just as happy as Sam and Alice next door. I say, if it is O.K. for them to be alright, then it is O.K. for me to be alright too. You do not have to have the same things the people next door has in order to be alright. Do what makes you happy. Do your thing; your own way. Again, it has been my pleasure to come to you. I want you to know that I live and have lived. I want America and the world to know that I care for my neighbors. I have shared with you the best of myself and I hope you will grow or have grown from reading of my experiences. I hope the best for you, always. Also, I want the world to know that I care for the well-being of the children around the world. I have given you the last scroll. Also, I want the world to know that I am my brother's keeper.

The world may not care for you; I do. I hope you will take this scroll and begin a new life. A life time of prosperity is waiting for you. Therefore, embrace every moment of your life while there is still time. Wait no longer. Again, the ultimate decision is yours. My question to you is, will you choose to live or do you want to continue on down the road to destruction? I pray always that you now decide to take this scroll and redirect your life. I tell you; death does not discriminate. The chilly wind of death lurks wheresoever it is commanded; by God. No one knows when that wind will blow again. You can be here one moment and in a split second, be gone the next moment. Again, will you be ready? Are you prepared or preparing to exit this life? Are you ready to stand before your Maker? I am ready and I hope by the end of this novel, you will be ready as well. I hope you will take heed to this scroll. A new beginning awaits you.

The short story at the beginning was fictitious, the story was just an example of how good and evil can interact in our lives. For the most part of this novel, the writings are based on true events. I have written this novel with seriousness and I hope you will take the contents serious. I have given you some of the best experiences of my life that I know. You will perhaps never again read such a novel as this one. The Last Scroll was written to give you hope. For hope is the corner stone to building a new life. Your faith is the last stone by which you complete the building. Consider your life as a newly constructed building. Build with confidence and you will receive the desired result. Take this novel and use it to the best of your ability. You are a winner! Trust always in the Lord Jesus Christ or whomever you choose to believe in and seek a new beginning. The Lord stands before you with open arms. Will you now run into His open arms? Farewell my friends, farewell! Continue to pray for me as I do for you and all others.

THE END.

www.ingramcontent.com/pod-product-compliance
Lightning Source LLC
LaVergne TN
LVHW041853070526
838199LV00045BB/1571